THE
STORY
OF
TATA

THE STORY OF

1868 to 2021

TATA

The Story of the Family That Built a Global Empire

PETER CASEY

PENGUIN
VIKING

An imprint of Penguin Random House

VIKING

USA | Canada | UK | Ireland | Australia
New Zealand | India | South Africa | China | Singapore

Viking is part of the Penguin Random House group of companies
whose addresses can be found at global.penguinrandomhouse.com

Published by Penguin Random House India Pvt. Ltd
4th Floor, Capital Tower 1, MG Road,
Gurugram 122 002, Haryana, India

First published in Viking by Penguin Random House India 2021

Copyright © Peter Casey 2021

All rights reserved

12 11

The views and opinions expressed in this book are the author's own and the
facts are as reported by him, which have been verified to the extent possible,
and the publishers are not in any way liable for the same.

ISBN 9780670090228

Typeset in Adobe Caslon Pro by Manipal Technologies Limited, Manipal
Printed at Thomson Press India Ltd, New Delhi

www.penguin.co.in

Contents

Contents

Dedication

This book is dedicated to the people who were instrumental in protecting the Tata flame and keeping it alive. All played a critical role and none was more important than the other. Without these amazing people, the Tata flame would not have survived, the amazing company that is Tata Sons would not exist and the impact that they have had on India and the world would never have happened. There have been eight key protectors thus far. They are, in chronological order:

1. **Jamsetji Tata (1839–1904):** The visionary who lit the flame.
2. **Sir Dorabji Tata (1859–1932):** The second chairman of Tata, whose commitment to fulfilling his father's dreams should qualify him for the title of the most important protector.
3. **Sir Ratanji Tata (1871–1918):** Ironically, it was his premature death at forty-seven that changed the evolution of Tata. His will established the Sir Ratanji Tata Trust, the first major trust, which forever changed the face of business in India. His death also led to Lady Navajbai adopting Naval.
4. **Sir Nowroji Saklatwala (1875–1938):** The first chairman not to be called Tata. A distant cousin of Jamsetji, Sir Nowroji led Tata Sons through the Great Depression and was a stabilizing influence. His sudden death led to the unexpected elevation of JRD.

5. **Lady Navajbai Tata (1887–1965):** Lady Navajbai has many reasons to be included as a protector of the flame. She adopted Naval and would go on to become a Tata Sons board member for over forty years. She also helped raise Naval's two sons with Soonoo, Ratan and Jimmy, and had a profound influence on them both, particularly on Ratan.

6. **J.R.D. Tata (1904–93):** JRD ran Tata Sons for more than fifty years and saw the complete transformation and globalization of the company. His generosity in giving his siblings an equal share of the shares in Tata Sons, which was left to him by his father, R.D. Tata, would go on to prove that no good deed ever goes unrewarded.

7. **Naval Tata (1904–89):** Randomly chosen from an orphanage and delivered into a life of unimaginable wealth. He went through a very challenging divorce, at a time when divorces were very rare. A huge influence on the way Tata Sons evolved and adapted to the changing times after Independence, he served on the board of Tata Sons for more than forty years and was a constant foil and buffer to JRD. Elected seven times to the board of the International Labour Organization, his political savvy helped guide Tata Sons during turbulent times.

8. **Ratan Tata (1937–Present):** The only person to ever be chairman of Tata Sons and chairman of both major trusts. He grew Tata Sons exponentially. He made major acquisitions, such as Tetley Tea, Corus Steel and Jaguar Land Rover, which completely changed the footprint of Tata Sons. He also led the company at arguably the two most challenging times in the history of Tata Sons, the terrorist attack on the Taj Mahal Palace Hotel and the removal of the chairman of Tata Sons, Cyrus Mistry.

Natarajan Chandrasekaran, commonly known as Chandra, was born in 1963. Chandra is the person selected to be the chairman of

Tata Sons after Cyrus Mistry was removed. It is far too early in his tenure to classify him as a protector of the flame. During his time at the helm so far, he has been impressive.

Although **Cyrus Mistry** was on the Tata board for a total of eleven years—six as a member, one as vice chairman and four as chairman—it is unlikely that he would qualify as a protector of the flame.

List of Abbreviations

AMP	Advanced Management Program
ASPCA	American Society for the Prevention of Cruelty to Animals
BDC	Bombay Dyeing Company
BSE	Bombay Stock Exchange
CSR	Corporate social responsibility
HBS	Harvard Business School
JLR	Jaguar Land Rover
NCDs	Non-convertible debentures
NCLAT	National Company Law Appellate Tribunal
NELCO	National Radio and Electronics Company
TCI	Tata-Cornell Institute for Agriculture and Nutrition
TCS	Tata Consultancy Services
TELCO	Tata Engineering and Locomotive Company
TISCO	Tata Iron and Steel Company Limited
TKS	TELCO Kamgar Sanghatana

Acknowledgements

One of the problems of singling out people to thank is that you inevitably leave someone out. At his golden wedding anniversary dinner, my first mentor, my grandfather, went to great lengths to thank everyone who had come a long way to help him and my grandmother celebrate, and he forgot to mention the lady sitting beside him—his sister and only surviving sibling of twelve. So, if I leave anyone out, my profuse apologies.

This book would not have been possible had it not been for the many wonderful hours I spent conversing with Ratan Tata himself, which he very graciously allowed me to record. Ratan's half-brother, Noel, also was kind enough to spend time with me and gave me a different insight into their father, Naval. Over the years, I have spent many hours with the senior executives of Tata, including the new chairman, Chandra. I also met with Venkat (R. Venkataramanan), the manager of the Tata Trusts. Mr N.A. Soonawala was also very generous with his time.

It would not have been possible if my wife and the mother of my five wonderful children—Fionnbarr, Ryan, Neala, Ailisha and Siofra—had not been so very able and willing to pick up the pieces and hold the family together as I globe-trotted around the world. So, a huge thank-you to Helen.

It just proves the adage, 'You are never too old to make new friends.' (I am referring to myself and Ratan, not Helen.)

Almost twenty years ago, I got a phone call that changed my life. It was from Gabriel Rozman, who, at the time, was running Latin America for Ernst & Young. He said that he was leaving E&Y and joining a company called Tata. This was long before Google, and it took me some time to learn about Tata and the division he was joining, called Tata Consultancy Services. Gabby was a very highly respected senior partner in the firm, and I was completely confused. Capgemini had just bought the consulting division of E&Y, and he had decided to leave to join a company I had never heard of. He explained that Tata was an Indian company and that they had a consulting division and that he was going to be heading 'Ibero-America', which I later found out was Latin America and every country that spoke Portuguese or Spanish.

That phone call changed my life. It brought Tata into my life. It brought the Zoroastrian religion into my life. It caused me to become fascinated by a whole new way of doing business. So, another huge thank-you goes to Gabby.

It was Gabby who introduced me to Chandra, who, at the time, was essentially COO of TCS. Chandra's combination of passion and personal discipline had a huge impact on me. I started working out again and getting up earlier. So, thank you, Chandra.

Finally, and I have left many key important contributors out, Rajendra Prasad Narla, at the Tata Archives, was an invaluable supporter and corrector of my many errors. I had many people who read and corrected my grammar, and context, such as Patrick Durkan and Alan Axelrod and Meru Gokhale at Penguin Random House, but I take full responsibility for the errors they missed!

Prologue

The Flame Kindled

In a free enterprise, the community is not just another stakeholder in business but is in fact the very purpose of its existence.
—Jamsetji Nusserwanji Tata, founder of Tata Group[1]

The Tata Group is huge, with some 660,000 employees and a broad, palpable global footprint. Yet it is seldom recognized for what it truly is—an alternative to conventional capitalism. Call it a 'Third Way'. It is a kind of capitalism that is far from the traditional meaning of the word. It tries to address issues that Karl Marx and other thinkers have raised, but certainly not in the same way as communism has. Third Way? In truth, it is 'the Tata Way'.

The Tata Way is a middle path to both conventional capitalism and its other extreme, Marxism. It not only attempts to solve many of the discontents of capitalism, as conventionally practised, but has also proven itself a practical alternative to Marxism, which has been tried and has failed over and over again, for about the past 150 years. Despite this, the Tata Way—the unique profitable/philanthropic model that the Tata Group embraces—is hardly known at all, at least not outside of India. While much of Western economic, social, political and moral thought has been informed, if not dominated, by Karl Marx's reproachful analysis of capitalism ever since the late 19th century, the Tata alternative, which began with the company's founder, Jamsetji Tata, and his two sons, has hardly been given a voice, let alone a hearing.

Ratan Tata, a distant relative of Jamsetji Tata, has observed, 'Marx's vision was to take from the rich to feed the poor. Jamsetji's vision was to make the poor rich.'[2] Karl Marx has been long dead, but he has left behind his intellectual legacy. Jamsetji Tata and his sons, Dorabji and Ratanji, have likewise departed this dimension without having written a single book. Yet Jamsetji brought industry to India and founded in 1868 what is now a company with (as of 2017) revenues of $100.4 billion, assets of $126 billion and a workforce of about 695,000.[3] The range of the Tata Group's enterprises is staggering: from airlines to automobiles, aerospace, defence products, consumer packaged goods, chemicals and consulting. In addition, Tata companies provide electric power and broadband service. They are also in healthcare, engineering, real estate and finance. They make locomotives and vehicles of all kinds. And they make steel, with a global presence in the steel industry across five continents. As the Indians like to put it, Tata is a 'salt-to-software conglomerate'.

The first two generations of Tatas built businesses, which became a great conglomerate of remarkable companies. These in turn became national assets, which further led to the foundation of even greater companies. Making a profit is *necessary* to capitalism, but, in the Tata founders' vision of capitalism, it is not *sufficient*. The family's ancient Zoroastrian faith taught them the duty of creating real happiness by improving the lives of others.

Interestingly, Ratan Tata's view is that Jamsetji did not build his business empire as a family business. He was a visionary with the courage to build major industrial world-class ventures, manned by expatriates in the first instance, which were essential for a developing nation. He built a steel plant because a developing nation needed to have the ability to produce steel—the basic industrial material. He invested in a textile mill because Indian cotton was being exported to the UK, being woven into cotton textiles and re-exported back to India. Jamsetji wanted India to be self-sufficient. He similarly envisaged a hydel power plant to provide electricity to the city of Bombay (now Mumbai) and a modern world-class hotel to create a luxurious environment for visitors. He did all this for the nation—not for his family.

He believed in the generation of profit and the creation of wealth to fulfil his national vision. He expected his sons, Dorabji and Ratanji, to fulfil his industrial dreams and grow his industrial empire with the same values, ethics and excellence that he had envisaged for these industries. Jamsetji's industrial dreams were fatefully fulfilled by his two sons, who had no children. They left their personal wealth (in the form of ownership in the industrial empire created by Jamsetji) in two philanthropic trusts. There, the profits from the industrial ventures would be ploughed back for the better good of the community and the downtrodden, through the creation of educational institutions and other entities for social uplift in the areas of education, medical facilities and rural progress.

For Jamsetji, his immediate goal of creating businesses of national importance was inseparable from his concern for the community. 'In a free enterprise,' Jamsetji wrote, 'the community is not just another stakeholder in business but is in fact the very purpose of its existence.'[4] In common usage in the West, the phrase 'free enterprise' is virtually synonymous with 'capitalist,' and we may therefore take his use of the phrase as a bold and straightforward affirmation of Jamsetji's belief in the virtues of capitalism. Yet, for him, capitalism should be embraced among its stakeholders more than owners and investors. 'Very first' among the stakeholders of a 'free enterprise', as Jamsetji defined it, is 'the community'.

Extolling the unique feature of Tata is not intended to belittle the likes of other philanthropic enterprises, such as the Bill & Melinda Gates Foundation. Without question, it is a mammoth philanthropic wonder. Yet it is very different from the Tata model. The purpose of the foundation is to give away the enormous wealth created by the Gates and Warren Buffet. In this, it follows the philosophy of Andrew Carnegie, the ruthless steel magnate of America's 'Gilded Age', who, in 1901, published an essay called 'The Gospel of Wealth'. The 'duty of the man of wealth', he wrote, was 'to set an example of modest, unostentatious living, shunning display or extravagance', providing 'moderately for the legitimate wants of those dependent upon him', and then using 'all surplus revenues . . . as trust funds' to be used in ways he believed would 'produce the most beneficial results for the community'. If the wealthy did their duty, Carnegie wrote, 'we shall have an ideal state, in which the surplus wealth of the few will become, in the best sense the property of the many, because administered for the common good'. Those who fail to allocate their surplus wealth in this manner while living suffer a fate Carnegie summed up in a single memorable sentence: 'The man who dies thus rich dies disgraced.'[5]

Carnegie and his modern successors, such as Gates and Buffett, began their giving while they lived and took a personal hand in guiding their charitable investments. But Jamsetji Tata and the keepers of the flame who followed him were far more radical. They created and grew a company that is ultimately unique in the world. Tata Sons, the holding company for the conglomerate, has an array of companies that include privately held and publicly traded enterprises, yet they are, in essence, all owned by a philanthropic trust. The companies work hard every day to make money so they can give back to their investors while promoting the philanthropic goals of their founders. This is what makes the story of Tata worth telling.

To tell it, one has to research it—to the extent possible, first-hand. Many Tata Sons leaders contributed directly and some indirectly to this book. They include:

Ratan Tata	Chairman Emeritus of Tata Sons and chairman of the Sir Ratanji Tata Trust and the Sir Dorabji Tata Trust, and the associated trusts
Cyrus Mistry*	Former chairman of Tata Sons and former CEO of Shapoorji Pallonji Group and 50 per cent owner
Madhu Kannan	Former CEO of the BSE and member of the Tata Sons Global Executive Committee
Natarajan Chandrasekaran	Chairman of Tata Sons and former CEO of TCS
Mukund Rajan	Former member of Global Executive Committee and brand custodian of Tata Sons
N.A. Soonawala	Former vice-chairman of Tata Sons
F.C. Kohli	Former CEO and founder of TCS
S. Ramadorai	Long-time CEO of TCS
S. Padmanabhan	Former global head of HR for TCS and former COO of Tata Power
Noel and Aloo Tata	Noel is Ratan's half-brother. CEO of Trent and CEO of Tata International and a member of the Tata Trusts. Aloo, his wife, is Cyrus Mistry's sister.
Nupur Mallick	Global head of HR for Tata Sons
Rajesh Gopinathan	CEO of TCS
Rajendra Prasad Narla	Tata archivist
Harish Bhat	Brand custodian for Tata Sons

* Cyrus Mistry declined to be interviewed for this book.

In addition to the above, more than fifty senior people who had knowledge of the events that unfolded contributed to telling the Tata story. Some, like Ratan, were happy to be recorded, while some preferred to speak but not be named. In all, their insights were invaluable.

The purpose of this book is not to 'knock' or criticize any particular party. The purpose is to give a deeper understanding of the events that led to one of the most amazing days in Indian business. Most of the books and articles written so far have been very one-sided, presenting Cyrus's version of events.

The truth is that CEOs and chairmen get fired all the time in the US and Europe. One can argue about whether a particular leader deserves dismissal or not, but the one thing that everyone agrees with is that once the board of a company has lost confidence in its chairman or CEO, it is in everyone's best interests that they part ways. This would certainly have been the preferred option for the board of Tata Sons. They had lost confidence in the leadership of Cyrus Mistry, he was dismissed and the world moved on. To understand why this preferred outcome did not occur, we must put together all the interconnected pieces in a puzzle in which the pieces have been joining one to another since 1868, when Jamsetji Tata decided to set up a company that would change not just India but indeed the world.

1

'Go on Doing My Work and Increasing It'

'Cyrus Mistry fired!' exclaimed the India.com headline on 24 October 2016. Calling the move 'extremely unexpected' and its impact 'shocking',[1] the article announced the seemingly sudden ouster of the chairman of Tata Sons.

No Indian company is more iconic than Tata, the nation's largest conglomerate, founded in 1868 by one of India's national heroes, Jamsetji Tata. Composed of more than 130 separate firms, Tata has long been a source of tremendous pride for India. What made the news of the shake-up at the top more disturbing was that there was little public sign of trouble before that fateful day in October. There was no public scandal, no publicized act of gross mismanagement, no instance of 'proven corruption' prior to the 'sacking' of the Tata Group chairman. As NDTV put it, the event came 'without any prior warning or signal'. Amid 'shock waves both at home and abroad', NDTV asked: 'What triggered . . . the removal of Mr Mistry?'[2]

Chairmen and CEOs get fired all the time, but in India, 24 October 2016 will be remembered as one of the most significant in the history of business—certainly the most significant in India. That was the day that Cyrus Mistry was asked to step aside as the chairman of Tata Sons, the role he had only held for four years.

Since its founding in 1868, there had only been five previous chairmen of Tata Sons. None had ever been fired. Three had died in office, and the other two, J.R.D. Tata and Ratan Tata, were eighty-six and seventy-five, respectively, when they retired, so it certainly came as a shock to some in the business community when Mistry was relieved of his responsibilities at the relatively young age of fifty.

In the short time since Mistry was relieved of control, books have been written and many-thousand words committed to print, all presenting different versions of the events that led up to his firing. Some are more accurate than others.

The net net, however, is that when an organization's board of directors loses confidence in its chairman and/or CEO, it is always time for a separation. That said, there was no one factor that caused the board to lose confidence in Mistry's leadership. There were many issues—some small, others large, all significant—that, taken together, forced the board to act.

To fully understand how the events of Mistry's rise, tenure as chairman and dismissal unfolded, you have to understand the dynamics and complexities of how businesses at the highest levels in India operate. This book is an attempt to give the reader a more comprehensive picture of all of the events, all the forces leading up to that momentous event. It explains, as factually and objectively as possible, the backgrounds of the key players and organizations.

To appreciate the significance of the removal of Cyrus Mistry from the most influential position in business, we must understand how the House of Tata came to exist in the first place. This requires comprehending the dynamics and the intricate relationships that existed between several family dynasties—the Tatas, the Dinshaws, the Wadias and the Mistrys.

The Mistry and Tata families became inextricably intertwined in 1936, when Cyrus Mistry's grandfather, Shapoorji Pallonji Mistry, bought 17.5 per cent of Tata Sons, the Tata principal holding company.

Shapoorji's father, Pallonji, was a builder. He was industrious but not yet wealthy in the 1860s, when Nusserwanji Tata and Dadabhoy Tata (his cousin and brother-in-law) were embarking on trade with China. The Tatas soon became prosperous, in contrast to the Mistrys of that time.

It was only after Shapoorji founded Shapoorji Pallonji & Co. and progressed from being a journeyman builder to an increasingly high-powered contractor, building homes for Bombay's elite, that his fortune began to change. Among the wealthiest clients of Shapoorji Pallonji & Co. was Framroze Edulji Dinshaw, a prominent attorney, landowner and financier.

During the 1920s, Dinshaw became closely associated with the Tatas, both business-wise and on a personal level. Impressed with Bombay House, Tata's headquarters, Framroze called on its architect, George Wittet, to design a house for him in Poona (now Pune). A banker friend advised Dinshaw to contract the building of the great house to Shapoorji Pallonji & Co. and, in the course of this work, Shapoorji Pallonji Mistry and Framroze Edulji Dinshaw became friends and business associates.

As the relationship between Mistry and Dinshaw crystallized, the Tatas pushed forward their vision for industrializing India. In this enterprise, Dinshaw became an indispensable source and broker of finance.

The Mistrys were not the only major Tata stakeholders who were not direct descendants of Jamsetji Tata. Sylla Tata, the sister of J.R.D. Tata, who was the longest-serving chairman of Tata Group (serving from 1938 to 1991), married Sir Dinshaw Petit.

Born in Liverpool, England, in 1911 (and who died in Bombay in 1996), Neville Wadia was educated at Malvern College and Trinity College, Cambridge. He joined his father's textile business, Bombay Dyeing, in 1933, and rose to its chairmanship in 1952. He retired a quarter-century later, having led the company to great success as one of India's largest textile producers. It was considered the flagship of the Wadia Group, one of India's oldest conglomerates, having been founded by Sir Lovji Nusserwanjee Wadia in 1736 as a builder of ships for the British East India Company.

Neville Wadia was instrumental in the growth of the Indian textile industry and founded the Cotton Textiles Export Promotion Council, which he led for twelve years. His philanthropic works included building new wings and upgrading several hospitals in Mumbai that had been founded by his family. He himself founded a college of commerce in Pune, (120 miles) south of Mumbai. He also founded numerous Parsi charitable trusts. With his wife, Dina, he had a child, Nusli Wadia, who came to play an important role in modern Tata history. Dina's father was Muhammad Ali Jinnah, the founder of Pakistan.

~

Before we return to the further evolution of the Tata family, let us first understand that, for all the attention long focused on Tata in India, there is a serious misconception that the Tata family controls the Tata Group. In fact, the Tata family have, over several generations, given away their ownership of Tata Sons, the holding company for the group. To be sure, the Tata Group is still typically referred to as a 'family company'—a description that creates the expectation of a certain simplicity, both of structure and evolution, as the torch is passed from father to children, generation after generation. However, that is misleading, as both the structure and evolution of the Tata organization have been far more complex than what the 'family' label would imply.

Yet the founding spirit of Jamsetji Tata still pervades and animates the Tata companies.

Why?

In large part, this is the result of the impact of religion on the evolution of the House of Tata. The modern *Tata Code of Conduct & Ethics* firmly guides how companies within the Tata Group must operate. Clients and employees must be treated with respect and dignity, and, of course, discrimination of any nature is not tolerated. But to understand the enduring Tata culture requires understanding what motivated the founder, Jamsetji Tata, and his successors.

Jamsetji was a passionate and religious man. He was a Parsi, a devout Zoroastrian. Zoroastrianism is one of the oldest monotheistic religions in the world, and Jamsetji believed that one's admission to 'heaven' depended on how much one improved the lives of others. He instilled this Zoroastrian altruism in his two sons, who inherited their philanthropic traits from him.

Nusserwanji Tata (1822–86) was operating a trading firm in Navsari, a town in Gujarat hailed as the 'Jewel of the West', when Jamsetji was born to him and his wife, Jeevanbai, on 3 March 1839. He would be the only son of five children.

Nusserwanji broke with family tradition by becoming a businessman instead of joining the Zoroastrian priesthood like his father and his father's father before him. An early biographer of Jamsetji tells us that, as a youngster, Nusserwanji earned a reputation as 'a sharp lad, able, resourceful, and intelligent', with a 'natural shrewdness' that 'counterbalanced his lack of education'. These traits made him restless, and he was never 'long content with . . . modest opportunities. Honest and frugal . . . he saved a little money which soon enabled him to become the first of his family to do business on an extensive scale'.

That Nusserwanji had gone into business instead of priesthood did not mean that he had renounced his religion. For one thing, he continued to make his home in Navsari. Located in the coastal lowland, the town lies alongside the Purna River, amid fields of sugarcane, chikoo plantations and mangoes. Navsari is a very old place, having been founded a thousand years before the year 1141, when Zoroastrians who had emigrated from Persia first settled in the town. As Persian émigrés, they were called 'Parsis'. The Parsi influence pervaded Navsari, which, during Jamsetji's early years, was a kind of religious headquarters for the Parsi Zoroastrians, who kept the holy fire, which was originally lit in Sanjan when the first Parsis arrived in Gujarat, burning for some 300 years before it was moved to Udvada, where it burns to this day. Keeping the flame of the faith burning is essential to Zoroastrianism and the Parsi community.[3]

Within the whole of India, the Parsis were never a large community, not even within Navsari, but they made their mark nevertheless, and Navsari stood as a centre of religious culture and learning. The values of the faith were inescapable, and trader-entrepreneur Nusserwanji Tata passed those values down to Jamsetji, who in turn passed them down to his sons, Ratanji and Dorabji.

Paramount among these values was the duty of lifting others from suffering and improving their lives. Among Zoroastrians, it is through the performance of this duty that a person makes themselves righteous and thus worthy of heaven.[4]

The tradition in the Tata family was that the eldest son would become a Zoroastrian priest. Jamsetji followed his father's example, rather than that of his earlier ancestors, in pursuing not a priestly calling but a business career. It was certainly not a departure from Parsi tradition. As R.M. Lala has observed, a 'renaissance seems to have taken hold of the Parsis around 1850 which resulted in the flowering of their creativity and genius on all fronts', with commerce among them.[5] Parsis had long been merchants, but by the mid-19th century the Parsi merchant class was on the rise.

Clearly, young Jamsetji Tata was caught up in this Parsi 'renaissance'. Once he was of age, his parents enrolled him in the local *gurukul* (school). Especially impressed by the boy's facility in mathematics, his father hired a private tutor in the subject.[6] He showed such promise as a student both in the gurukul and with his tutor that, after Nusserwanji moved his business to Bombay (today Mumbai) and expanded into banking and international trade, he sent for thirteen-year-old Jamsetji in 1853 and, the following year, enrolled him in the capital's newly opened Elphinstone College, one of the earliest and most important products of the 'Parsi renaissance'. It would educate generations of young Indians in the tradition of British-influenced Victorian intellectual liberalism.[7]

As R.M. Lala observes, 'Education . . . became the key to the Parsi flowering.'[8] For Jamsetji, it was also a flowering of another kind. While studying at Elphinstone, he met and subsequently married Hirabai Daboo, a young girl of the priestly class, the daughter of Cursetji Daboo.[9] Jamsetji was in his late teens at the time of India's First War of Independence, which the British Raj preferred to call the Sepoy Mutiny or the Indian Mutiny. It was in fact not so much a rebellion against the British Crown as against the rule of the British East India Company, which, in effect, represented British sovereign power in India. Yet it was the first serious challenge to the British Raj. Some historians even see it as the birth of the Independence movement in India.

However, it is likely that aspiring Indian merchants and entrepreneurs such as Jamsetji saw it less as a rebellion against the British Empire and more against the unfair monopoly the British East India Company enjoyed, which cramped the development of *Indian* business. Thus, in an early stage in his life, Jamsetji lived through an event that united commerce, nationalism and entrepreneurial possibilities with independence. In the end, although the Sepoy Mutiny was suppressed and therefore unsuccessful, the unfolding social and political drama likely stirred in young Jamsetji his early nationalist sentiment. It may have led him to believe that Indian economic self-sufficiency was a necessary prerequisite to anything approaching independence. The reverse was also true: a commercially strong India would have a better chance of achieving nationhood.

An early biographer wrote of young Jamsetji's 'industry and quickness of mind', which he called 'remarkable'. At Elphinstone, it was noted, that so 'absorbed was [Jamsetji] in his work that he left little impression upon his fellow-students, and confined his acquaintance to a very small circle'. But that circle was distinctive. As an adult, Jamsetji 'gave an annual dinner for the Elphinstonians of his day', which included the likes of the great Indian scholar and social reformer Sir Ramkrishna Bhandarkar and Dinshaw Edjuli Wacha, a Parsi politician who became one of the founders of the Indian National Congress, of which he served as president.[10]

Jamsetji came out of Elphinstone as a 'green scholar'—a graduate with the equivalent of a bachelor's degree—in 1858. He had intended on going into one of the professions and even worked for a brief period in a solicitor's office, but his father needed him in his business, and so in 1859, he entered the firm of Nusserwanji and Kaliandas, general merchants. The company had made a good profit as contractors for the Anglo-Indian army. Jamsetji quickly gained experience with a wide variety of commodities and markets. He attributed the speed with which he mastered the complex business of commodities trading and markets to his liberal education. Within a few months of joining the firm, he was sent to Hong Kong to develop the China trade for the company. In December 1859, he was able to open a branch of the firm in that city under the name of Jamsetji and Ardeshir. The offices he opened in Holywood Road were occupied by the company's successors for some fifty years.[11]

Jamsetji and Ardeshir dealt principally in cotton and opium, which were high-margin goods. The partners sent back to India consignments of tea, silk goods, camphor, cinnamon, copper, brass and Chinese gold. A few months after establishing the

Hong Kong operation, Jamsetji travelled to Shanghai, where he quickly established another branch of the company. During his time in Shanghai, Jamsetji volunteered for service in the local militia while devoting himself to learning the ins and outs of the Eastern markets.[12]

Jamsetji Tata returned to India in 1863, only to find that Bombay was careening towards financial crisis. The United States Civil War (1861–65) created an acute shortage of cotton textiles, partly because the cotton-producing states of the Confederacy were confronted with a Union naval blockade, which made export very difficult. On top of that, some of the textile mills of England, whose owners opposed slavery, boycotted southern cotton. As a result, India became the prime exporter of raw cotton to the textile mills of Lancashire.

As the price of cotton rose, the Indian merchants' profits skyrocketed. The firm of Nusserwanji and Kahandas was among many that speculated wildly, placing their bets on the belief that the boom would last forever. Inundated with profit, one of Nusserwanji's partners, Premchand Roychand, speculated in land and in the creation of something called the Asiatic Banking Corporation. Its rapid success spurred the creation of other banks, and, as F.R. Harris put it, 'Money was lent upon every class of security, and though the Bombay Chamber of Commerce uttered a warning note, the warning passed unheeded.'[13]

Despite the warning signs and the actual warnings, Premchand Roychand asked Jamsetji to take ship for London and establish there an agency for his firm. He sailed early in 1864 with a twofold mission. He was to look after the shipments of Indian cotton arriving in Liverpool, and he was to establish the London branch of the Asiatic Banking Corporation. He carried with him a good many securities, and while he was still at sea, the markets began to crack. The bills he was carrying depreciated daily, and by the time he arrived in England, they were close to worthless. Jamsetji immediately cabled his firm to sell their cotton at once, but management was determined to hold out for what they believed would be a turnaround. Very shortly after Jamsetji landed in England, Premchand Roychand failed.[14]

Jamsetji Tata found himself thousands of miles from home, penniless. He pounded the pavement and knocked on doors until he was able to cobble together a number of local businesses willing to hire him as a liquidator. With his immediate financial needs addressed, Jamsetji used his spare time to make valuable connections in London's financial district as well as among the small but influential Parsi community in the capital.[15] When he was not doing his liquidation work, he travelled to Lancashire to oversee the arrival of the final cotton shipments. Eager to learn about the textile industry, he arranged to take several tours of mills in Lancashire and Manchester before returning to Bombay—just in time to help Premchand Roychand and his own father salvage as much of their business as possible.

Both despite and because of the difficulties Jamsetji faced in four years spent in England—which would prove to be only the first of several sojourns there—the varied strands of the young man's life began to come together in new ways. His knowledge of international trade and his growing responsibilities within his father's business were expanded with each new relationship he created among the expatriate Parsi community. He dealt regularly with Indian nationalists and left-leaning politicians, many of whom were very well connected with Prime Minister William Gladstone, the British liberal politician who had a hard-earned reputation as a defender of the poor.

His expanding circle within London brought Jamsetji into contact with socially liberal politics and the Indian nationalist movement. Each new relationship was another strand added to Jamsetji's intellectual, social and moral development. Each was in fact firmly tied to his spiritual roots.

Zoroastrianism was simultaneously spiritual and worldly. Not only was it bound up with commerce, which it fostered and encouraged, but, in contrast to Hinduism at the time, it did not forbid transoceanic travel. For these reasons, many in India's Parsi minority community became highly successful in business, including international trade. However, the religion's influence over Parsi business practices was not just a matter of allowing trade and travel. Zoroastrianism called on the faithful to consciously live their lives in ways intended to improve the world. The religion encouraged adherents to do well in business by doing good.[16]

Jamsetji was confident that the wheel of fortune would turn. He and his father had only to hold out. In 1867, the British government sent troops under Sir Robert Napier to liberate British subjects who had been imprisoned by the ruler of Abyssinia (modern Ethiopia). Nusserwanji Tata was able to secure the contract for supplying the British expeditionary force, and the quick profits made enabled Jamsetji's father to restore his lost wealth. As for Jamsetji, he used his portion of the Abyssinian expedition profits to make use of the knowledge he had acquired in touring the mills of Lancashire and Manchester. In London, he had learnt much about customer relations. In the mill cities, he studied, first-hand, the rapid spread and effect of the Industrial Revolution in England, and in 1869, he partnered with his father and a few others to purchase a bankrupt and derelict oil mill at Chinchpokli, today a neighbourhood in south Mumbai. They renamed it the Alexandra Mill in honour of the Princess of Wales and quickly converted it into a cotton mill, which Jamsetji managed, learning the business even as he led it. After two years, the Alexandra Mill was showing a decent profit, and Jamsetji sold it to a prominent mill owner and cotton merchant named Kesowji Naik.[17] His rationale for selling a profitable mill reveals much about Jamsetji's approach to business. A rapid profit was not his objective. What he wanted was to finance a new mill with the latest machinery. His orientation was towards the future, and his intention was to make India competitive in textiles on a global scale. That required the most modern equipment.

As Jamsetji saw it, creating the great textile works he wanted to build also called for wider and deeper knowledge of the state of the art of the cotton industry. Consequently, on 26 April 1873, he decided to set off from Bombay and sail yet again for England, this time for a closer study of the cotton industry in Lancashire, which was the global epicentre of the textile-manufacturing and coal-mining industries. His objective was not merely to follow the leader but to become competitive with it. He deliberately took the long way in his journey, stopping in Egypt, Syria, Palestine, Turkey and Russia.

If he was to trade with the world, he wanted to *see* the world and see it for himself. After studying cotton production in Lancashire, he returned to India and, in 1874, set up his new mill more than 500 miles inland from Bombay, in the central Indian city of Nagpur. The city's location in the heart of the subcontinent's cotton-growing country was a competitive advantage, but Nagpur was also remote from major infrastructure. As Jamsetji saw it, this deficiency gave him an opportunity to build something truly new, which is, he believed, precisely what India needed.

At the time Jamsetji set to work on the mill, India had barely entered the Industrial Revolution. There were already fifteen textile mills in Bombay, containing a total of 462,151 spindles, but these were very old buildings containing antiquated machinery. The working conditions were very poor—worse even than those of the mills Jamsetji had toured in the industrial slums of England. Indian labour was, of course, cheap—but it was also untrained, unskilled and poorly motivated.[18] Jamsetji was determined that his mill would begin to bring change to Indian industry.

He called the new enterprise the Central India Spinning, Weaving and Manufacturing Company. Less than three years later, on 1 January 1877, when Queen Victoria was proclaimed empress of India, Jamsetji renamed the company Empress Mills. It was a brilliant stroke of marketing. Far from defying the British Raj, it paid homage to the new empress—but at the same time, it was clearly an honour conferred by an *Indian* enterprise upon a *British* monarch. The message behind this was that an Indian business possessed the social, economic and political standing to confer a meaningful honour on a head of state. It was an assertion of a legitimate business competitor—an enterprise fit to compete with the best of Lancashire—and it was also an assertion of India's place in the global community.

Most important of all, the renaming of Empress Mills was a bold wager—that the enterprise would succeed and in a major way. If it failed, the failure would not just be personal. It would have, in its way, significance in the world, significance among the politicians and bureaucrats administering the Raj and a serious impact on India's future. But Jamsetji did not mean to fail, and indeed, by the time of the name change, his cotton company was very successful. This fact served only to spur Jamsetji to yet greater visions for his company.

Jamsetji Tata set four long-term corporate goals. The first was to build an iron and steel plant. The second was to bring hydroelectric power to India. The third, which was truly remarkable for the time, was to create a world-class institute of science in and for the nation. Beyond these, his fourth goal was to give to Bombay and to India a world-class hotel. His rationale for this project was that if India was to join the family of great industrial and mercantile nations, its chief city and centre of business needed to both attract and accommodate the world's movers and shakers. A world-class hotel would project a world-class image for the city and the nation. So he added a fourth vision, the Taj Mahal Palace Hotel. Sadly, it was the only one of his dreams that he lived to see to fruition. It opened in 1902, and he died in 1904.[19]

The idea for building the hotel came to Jamsetji, it is said, towards the end of the 19th century, when he took a foreign friend to lunch at the Watson Hotel, then Bombay's most elegant and today a ten-minute stroll from the Taj. Trouble was, as an Indian, Jamsetji was denied service in the all-white Watson. We don't know if he was embarrassed by this. (Unlikely.) We don't know if he was outraged. (Even less likely.) Indeed, we don't even know for certain if this incident really happened. But it is certain that he recognized Bombay's need for a hotel worthy of what he wanted the city to become: an international, cosmopolitan destination for Asians and Europeans and everyone else, regardless of nationality, religion or race. Designed by Indian architects— Sitaram Khanderao Vaidya and D.N. Mirza[20]—it would be an Indian hotel for the world.

As Jamsetji's Parsi tradition taught him to live so as to make the lives of others better, the Taj would greet travellers 'with the ethos *atithi devo bhava* (the guest is god)'.[21] For Jamsetji, the Taj was truly an act of faith. He invested Rs 26 million in its construction, the equivalent of GBP 200 million today, or roughly USD 250 million. As originally built, this sum paid for thirty sumptuous private apartments and 350 double and single rooms in what was India's first hotel with electric power (supplied by its own power plant), electric lighting, electric fans and electric clocks. And those fans were not the only means by which guests stayed cool. A cutting-edge precursor of modern air-conditioning, a CO_2-charged refrigeration system, both cooled the hotel and provided refrigeration for food; there was also an ice-making system to supply the hotel bar, the first licensed bar in the city.

The question was, would the hotel ever pay for itself?

Then again, this was probably not the question uppermost in Jamsetji's mind when he decided to build it.

When Ratan Tata was asked if he was concerned that, as the chairman of a family company, he might be tempted to make decisions to protect the family name, but which could compromise the business profitability, Ratan answered by shifting away from issues of money as well as family. 'You see, we've always been somewhat closer to national assets—building and operating national assets,' he said. These have included steel and power companies as well as the airline that became Air India, but the Taj was intended as a national asset as well. Its value and the way it was run went beyond the bounds of both a family business and a straightforward for-profit business. The good of the nation was bound up in it.

Ratan went on to explain that, as he saw it, 'the Tata organization has withstood the test of time in terms of its direction'. 'We're a group that stays with it. We fight through the difficult periods'.[22] When you operate national assets, you have a profound responsibility that must be taken very seriously.

And it can be a heavy burden, as Jamsetji discovered. When the Taj opened on 3 December 1903, the reviews were not good. Both the British and the upper-class Indian residents of Bombay turned up their noses. How could an Indian and an Indian company expect to run a first-class hotel? When he died on 19 May 1904, while on a business trip in Germany, Jamsetji had reason to believe that the Taj Mahal Palace Hotel would be remembered with scorn as his great folly. But before the first decade of the 20th century had ended, the hotel began attracting the cosmopolitan clientele the founder had envisioned and was well on its way to becoming an object of national pride and a Tata legend. Today, the five-star hotel has expanded to 2,000,000 square feet, 560 rooms, forty-four suites, seven restaurants and two bars, serviced by a staff of 1700, including thirty-five butlers. It is the jewel among an exclusive portfolio of 108 hotels in twelve countries.[23]

Jamsetji Tata was an Indian patriot and nationalist who believed
that industrialization, education and innovation were essential in
raising India to an honoured place in the global family of nations.
This nationalist vision had taken shape, in significant measure,
outside of India, during Jamsetji's first sojourn in London, where
his circle of acquaintances came to include a combination of Parsi
and other Indian expatriates as well as liberal British politicians
and social thinkers. His vision for India was not insular but
global, because he had become a citizen of the world. He travelled
extensively, which was very unusual in those days, especially as the
means of travel were physically very arduous. His life of travel took
a physical toll, and perhaps it is not surprising that he fell ill while
on an extended business trip.

Jamsetji Nusserwanji Tata died on 19 May 1904, at Bad
Nauheim, a German town known for its spas and sanitariums,
which attracted people seeking relief from intractable ailments
and pain. We know that his son Dorabji was with him as he
passed, because it was to him that Jamsetji spoke his final words.
Characteristically, they were about the business. 'If you cannot
make it greater, at least preserve it. Do not let things slide. Go on
doing my work and increasing it, but if you cannot, do not lose
what we have done.'[24]

~

Jamsetji's dying declaration was a passing of the torch. He asked
his sons for two things. The first was to make the business—'my
work'—bigger and greater. The second was, if it could not be made
greater, to 'preserve it' and 'not lose what we have done'. Jamsetji
wanted the flame he had lit to grow into a glorious productive,
innovative and benevolent bonfire. Even more important than
increasing the size of the flame, however, was simply keeping
the flame alive, preserving the ethos of a company founded on

the principles of compassion *and* capitalism—not at odds with one another but essential to one another. This idea, ethos and commitment are what Dorabji and Ratanji received from their father.

In accordance with both the letter and the spirit of his final words, the ownership of Jamsetji's family business, Tata & Sons, passed to Dorabji (later Sir Dorabji) and Ratanji (later Sir Ratanji). In 1904, the year of their father's death, Ratanji and Dorabji merged the firm they had inherited, Tata & Sons, with Tata & Co., a company that their cousin Ratanji Dadabhoy ('RD') Tata, owned. The resulting company was named, simply, Tata Sons. It remains the basis of the holding company at the heart of today's global conglomerate.

Jamsetji's two sons were not his only children. He had a daughter, Dhunbai, who died at an early age. His sons were born rather far apart—Dorabji on 27 August 1859 and Ratan on 20 January 1871. Dorabji's primary education was at the prestigious Proprietary High School (today the Fort and Proprietary High School) in Bombay.

In 1875, when he was sixteen, Dorabji set off for England, where he was privately tutored in preparation for enrolment in Gonville & Caius College, Cambridge, in 1877. After two years, he returned to Bombay, where he enrolled at St Xavier's College, earning a bachelor of arts degree in 1882. Armed with his degree, Dorabji put in two years as a journalist for the *Bombay Gazette* before joining the cotton division of his father's firm in 1884.

Jamsetji dispatched him to the French Indian colony of Pondicherry on the south-eastern coast of the subcontinent. His assignment was to ascertain whether building a cotton mill there would be profitable. He soon concluded that it would be, and set about getting the required government approvals. In doing so, he impressed his father by the speed with which he secured them. From Pondicherry, Dorabji was sent to Nagpur and the Empress

Mills, which Jamsetji had founded in 1877. He would learn the cotton business from the inside out.

On a business trip to Mysore, Jamsetji Tata met Dr Hormusji Bhabha, a distinguished Parsi who became the first Indian Inspector-General of Education of Mysore state. At the Bhabha home, Jamsetji met Hormusji Bhabha's only daughter, Meherbai, and was impressed. On his return to Bombay, he sent Dorabji to Mysore to call on the Bhabhas and meet Meherbai, with whom he had fallen in love at first sight. The two were wed in 1897. Dorabji was thirty-eight, Meherbai just eighteen.[25]

Twelve years younger than Dorabji, Ratanji Tata was educated at St Xavier's in Mumbai and then entered his father's firm. He married Navajbai Sett in 1893. Although they both married, neither Dorabji nor Ratanji[26] had children. In 1896, Jamsetji committed a great act of philanthropy by giving away a large portion of his wealth to help establish the Institute of Science and Technology in Bangalore (a project that he would not live to see built, but which his son Ratanji, in collaboration with the Indian government and the Maharaja of Mysore, would bring to completion in 1909). However, Jamsetji 'gave ownership of Tata & Sons to his two sons, not to charity. It was his two sons, Ratanji and Dorabji, who had no children, who each created charitable trusts to control the family businesses'.

'Jamsetji created the national institutes,' Ratan Tata stated. 'He hired key people. He created jobs. He did all those things. He also did some philanthropy of his own, and through the companies, he looked after the workers. He introduced benefits for workers such as sick leave and maternity leave. He uplifted the people living around the works. He raised the standard of living. He did all of those things, but it wasn't part of his philosophy to give philanthropy out of his ownership. In the end, he gave 85 per cent of his company to his sons, and it was his sons, childless, who left almost their entire holding to charitable trusts.'

With his customary frankness, Ratan wondered aloud: 'Would Jamsetji's sons have taken this nationalist business farther beyond the family, would they have put philanthropy at the heart of the capitalist enterprise they had inherited, if they had had children? We will never know.'

～

What we do know is that Jamsetji created a thriving company, which he passed down to his two sons. It was his sons, Ratanji and Dorabji, who created the trusts and gave them majority control over the capitalist enterprise. Jamsetji's sons shared in the huge fortune their father left them, and while the elder son, Dorabji, became the company's chairman, it was the younger, Ratanji, who created the first of the great permanent Tata Trusts, which were made possible by what their father had begun. Following Jamsetji's death in 1904, Ratanji took charge of business relating to the L'Union Fire Insurance Co. of Paris, of which Tata & Sons was the agent in India. He also managed the trading firm Tata & Co., which had far-flung branches in Kobe, Shanghai, Paris, New York and Rangoon, trading in cotton, yarn, silk, pearls and rice.[27]

Ratanji worked side by side with Dorabji in running the Tata businesses, but it was clear that his main interests were philanthropic. He was among the early champions of Mahatma Gandhi, when he took up the struggle against racism in South Africa. Ratanji supported him morally as well as financially, contributing Rs 125,000 in all to the cause. Gandhi acknowledged the magnitude of this gift, writing, 'That India has been roused is evident from the generous gift of Mr Ratanji Jamsetji Tata . . . He will probably be followed by other Indians. Parsis are known the world over for their generous gifts. Mr Tata has been true to that spirit of generosity.' At this time, Ratanji also befriended Gopal Krishna Gokhale, the great Indian social reformer and freedom

fighter. For a decade, he presented Gokhale's Servants of India
Society with annual gifts in the amount of Rs 10,000. The society
conducted welfare work among India's poor.[28]

In 1909, five years after Jamsetji's death, Ratanji was
instrumental in realizing his father's unfulfilled plan to build an
Indian Institute of Science in Bangalore. At the same time, he also
worked with Dorabji to build and operate the great Tata iron and
steel plant at Sakchi, in what is today part of the city of Jamshedpur,
Jharkhand, and he played a role in the hydroelectric project in the
Western Ghats in 1915. Together, these three projects achieved
the three major corporate goals Jamsetji had established.

In 1912, Ratanji founded the Ratan Tata Department of Social
Sciences and Administration at the London School of Economics.
Here he also endowed a Ratan Tata Chair at the London School
of Economics, to finance the study of conditions among the poorer
classes. These acts of philanthropy marked a difference between
him and his father, who focused his charitable work more narrowly
on India. Thus, Ratanji pointed the way towards the more global
compass of the later work of the Tata Trusts.

Ratanji Tata's wife, Navajbai Sett, was born on 23 September
1877, the younger daughter of Ardeshir Merwanji Sett, a member
of a prominent Parsi family descended from Neriosang Dhaval,
a great Persian scholar who achieved prominence among the
14th-century Persian refugees in India. The Setts were renowned
for their wealth and their philanthropy. Navajbai grew up in an
environment of both social responsibility and privilege, becoming
an accomplished young equestrian who enjoyed playing polo. After
her marriage to Sir Ratanji Tata in 1893, the couple continued to
live in a manner that blended the privilege of wealth with a zeal for
philanthropy and business.

Materially and intellectually rich, theirs was also a loving
life, spent part-time in England, among the luminaries of British
society and aristocracy. The suave Sir Ratanji and the charming

Lady Navajbai fit very comfortably into English society and quickly mixed with the British elite. Their connections extended to the very pinnacle, in the form of a friendship with no less than King George V and Queen Mary. In 1906, Ratanji—now Sir Ratan Tata—purchased York House in Twickenham, a forested and wealthy area of south-west London.[29]

Sir Ratan and Lady Navajbai improved the house, especially its grounds, on which they built a large Italianate fountain enhanced with statuary along the riverside part of the garden. The couple were art lovers, who decorated the house with a world-class collection of jade, a number of paintings and other items, all acquired in the course of their world travels. More than a collector, Sir Ratanji was a connoisseur and scholar. Although he acquired many European works of fine and decorative art, he was fascinated by the rich history of India. He provided funding for the first archaeological excavation at Pataliputra, which took place during 1913 through 1917 under the direction of A.B. Spooner. The most spectacular find here was the hundred-column Mauryan throne room in the palace of the legendary King Ashoka. As for the European works he collected—paintings, specimens of military armaments, silverware, manuscripts, carpets, and more—these were gifted to the Prince of Wales Museum in Bombay. His intention was ultimately to move the collection to a new home he planned to build in Bombay, in partial emulation of the summer palace at Versailles. Alas, his premature death, on 5 September 1918, at St Ives, Cornwall, England, put an end to the plan of the couple living together in the new Bombay house. He was just forty-seven years old. His remains were transported to London, however, for burial beside his father, Jamsetji, at Brookwood Cemetery, Woking, near London.

The magnificent Bombay home, planned in 1912 and completed in 1915, stood waiting for Ratanji's widow, Lady Navajbai. Tata House, sometimes referred to as Tata Palace, is a majestic white building that is quite impossible to miss at Hazarimal

Somani Marg, Fort. It resembles a vast carving of ivory, glistening snow-white in the Mumbai sun. Its facade is exuberantly baroque, and the structure encloses an expansive courtyard. The terrace is lined with statues, which complete the impression of stately luxury. It became Lady Navajbai's home and was the place where Ratan Tata and his brother Jimmy grew up under her care. To this day, it is regarded as one of the finest buildings in Mumbai. As for the manor house in York, England, Lady Navajbai sold it in 1924, and the art collection, as her late husband had originally planned, went to the Prince of Wales Museum in Bombay (today, known as the Chhatrapati Shivaji Maharaj Vastu Sangrahalaya, Mumbai).

Ratanji died childless, which meant that the bulk of his fortune, except for a portion to sustain his widow, went to found the Sir Ratanji Tata Trust, which was endowed in 1919 with Rs 8 million. This was the first of the celebrated permanent Tata Trusts.

~

As mentioned, whereas Ratanji Tata put much of his energy and resources into philanthropic and social undertakings, his older brother, Dorabji, focused on the family business, serving as the second chairman of Tata Sons. Business, however, was not his only passion. He was an all-round sportsman and, in particular, a recognized equestrian. His enthusiasm for sport prompted him to become a major advocate for India's participation in the Olympics as early as 1919. It was 1920 before a 'provisional' Indian Olympic Committee was formed, and in 1927, the Indian Olympic Association was formally constituted under Dorabji's presidency.[30] Dorabji's advocacy came well in advance of the formation of an official Olympic committee. As Dorabji himself explained:

Having been educated in my youth in England, I had shared in nearly every kind of English athletics and acquired a great love for them. On my return to India I conceived the idea of introducing a love for such things there. I helped set up, with the support of English friends, a High School Athletic Association amongst numerous schools of Bombay, in the first place for cricket and then for athletics meetings, which embraced nearly all the events that form part of the Inter-University contests every year in London.[31]

For Dorabji, sport was an occasion for freely adopting European clothes, rules and notions of order and fair play. He was elected president of the Deccan Gymkhana, an athletics event that took place in Pune. When the gymkhana committee wanted to develop its sports programme in a manner more in line with established Indian traditions, Dorabji insisted on combining Indian and Western traditions, effectively fusing the two cultures. But there was one aspect of Indian culture that could not simply be fused to Western traditions. The Pune competitors were 'all boys of the peasant class working in the fields and living off poor fare'.[32] The organizers proposed to run their (100-yard) heats around a bend, without strings, because their sports ground was very small and the track was part of a rough unrolled grass field.

Dorabji admired that the gymkhana competitors could do so much with so little. In addition to the (100-yard) event, gymkhana staged a long-distance race of more than (25 miles), rightly designated as a marathon. Dorabji understood that the peasants who competed were accustomed to running barefoot on hard, macadamized or dirt roads. Indeed, despite their lack of training and the primitive track conditions, the first three or four men ran the distance in fair time. As Dorabji observed, it was a time that 'would compare well with the times done in Europe or elsewhere'.[33] This was no hollow boast. In 1919, some of the gymkhana performances were close to the times clocked by well-trained Western competitors in the Olympics.

It was, then, with high hopes that Dorabji decided to send three of the runners at his own expense to the Antwerp Games of 1920. The spirit of his peasant athletes was great, but Dorabji came to understand that spirit was not sufficient to compete on a global scale. His team had no conception of the standard of performance required to qualify for any of the events. For example, when a leading member of the gymkhana was asked what time he thought was standard for a (100-yard) race, he replied that it could be anything 'from half a minute to a minute'. He was astounded when told that an Olympic performance was not measured in minutes but in tenths of seconds. 'I hoped that with proper training and food, under English trainers and coaches, they might do credit to India. This proposal fired the ambition of the nationalist element in that city to try and send a complete Olympic team,' he later explained in a letter to the International Olympic Committee president, Count Baillet-Latour, in 1929.[34]

When Dorabji became president of the Indian Olympic Association, he financed the Indian team's participation in the 1924 Olympics in Paris out of his own pocket. His wife, Meherbai Tata, was a top tennis player who had won many national-level tournaments in the early 1920s. Loving husband though he was, Dorabji did not finance the team just to get his wife in. Sharing his father's nationalism, he believed there was great value in India fielding its own Olympic teams while still under the Raj. A matter of pride? Yes. But even more, it was an early gesture towards independence and thus an endeavour very much in the tradition of his father.

Dorabji's philanthropy and nationalism went far beyond his generosity in establishing India's place in the Olympics. In 1930, his wife, Lady Meherbai, was diagnosed with leukaemia, which claimed her life the following year. In early 1931, Dorabji placed virtually all of his wealth—over Rs 10 million (the equivalent of $64 million today), down even to his pearl-studded tiepin—in a trust, to be used 'without any distinction of place, nationality or creed, for the advancement of learning and research, the relief of distress, and other charitable purposes'.[35] In establishing the Sir Dorabji Tata Trust, he said:

> To my father, the acquisition of wealth was only a secondary object in life; it was always subordinate to the constant desire in his heart to improve the industrial and intellectual condition of the people of this country; and the various enterprises which he from time to time undertook in his lifetime had, for their principal object, the advancement of India in these important respects. Kind fate has, however, permitted me to help in bringing to completion his inestimable legacy of service to the country, and it is a matter of the greatest gratification to his sons to have been permitted to carry to fruition the sacred trust which he committed to their charge.[36]

Soon after establishing this trust, in April of the same year, as a memorial to his wife, he endowed the Lady Tata Memorial Trust with Rs 2.5 million (today, the equivalent of $16 million) to fund research into leukaemia. Additionally, the smaller Lady Meherbai D. Tata Education Trust was formed, partly from public donations, for the training of women in hygiene, health and social welfare.

Childless, like his brother, Sir Dorabji had no immediate family to inherit his wealth; therefore, the trustees of the Sir Dorabji Tata Trust were empowered to liquidate his lands, shares, securities and jewellery, including one particularly spectacular item. Extracted from the Jagersfontein Mine in the Orange Free State of South Africa and originally named the Reitz Diamond (after the state's President, Francis William Reitz), the gem weighed 245.35 carats, making it the largest diamond in the world at the time. (Today, it is the sixth-largest.) In 1897, it was renamed the Jubilee Diamond in honour of Queen Victoria's sixtieth year on the throne. Dorabji Tata bought the stone in about 1900 and presented it to Lady Meherbai. The trustees sold the gem, along with everything else they were empowered to sell, and established the Sir Dorabji Tata Trust. The only assets that were off-limits to the trustees were the shares Sir Dorabji held in Tata Sons.

Thus, it was Dorabji who created the next three great permanent Tata Trusts after the Sir Ratanji Tata Trust, which was established the year after Ratanji died. The Lady Tata Memorial Trust continues to fund research in leukaemia, while the Lady Meherbai D. Tata Education Trust supports advanced education for women. Among other activities, the Sir Dorabji Tata Trust supports the Tata Institute of Social Sciences, the Tata Memorial Centre for Cancer Research and Treatment, the Tata Institute of Fundamental Research, the National Centre for the Performing Arts, the National Institute of Advanced Studies and the Sir Dorabji Tata Centre for Research in Tropical Diseases.

~

It is natural to venerate Jamsetji Tata at the expense of his sons. The generally accepted view is that Jamsetji created the vision and that Dorabji and Ratanji did nothing more—or less—than take their late father's plans through execution. If true, this would be no small credit to him. But it is not accurate. Dorabji was far more than a mere lieutenant. He was a leader and a true visionary. He not only saw his father's unfinished dreams through realization but also, with Ratanji, improved them greatly.

In Bombay, Dorabji assumed the chairmanship, on Jamsetji's death in 1904, of the emerging conglomerate that had been renamed Tata Sons. He focused primarily on creating a modern iron and steel industry as well as a power industry in India. All of these exist today because of Dorabji's personal involvement and perseverance in their creation. What is more, Dorabji instigated and fostered expansion across the group. Under Dorabji's direction, three hydroelectric power companies were built, along with an oil and soap company, an insurance business and two cement companies.

Several years after taking over as chairman, Dorabji brought his cousin Ratanji Dadabhoy Tata (R.D. Tata), who was running a legal opium-trading business, into the family business. The combined entities were called Tata Sons. This combination has had repercussions which are still playing out to this day. R.D. Tata was given approximately 20 per cent of the combined entity.

R.D. Tata married a Parsi girl from the Banaji family, but she died young and without having borne any children. In his forties, R.D. Tata married Suzanne Brière (renamed Sooni in 1902), with whom he had five children—Rodabeh, Jehangir (JRD), Jimmy, Sylla and Darab. RD did not have the Midas touch of Sir Dorab when it came to making money and had to be bailed out personally by Sir Dorab. When he died in 1926, he left his shareholding and estate, including debts, which were owed to Sir Dorab, to his son Jehangir. Sir Dorabji at this time, was old, cranky and not in sound health or high spirits. He insisted that JRD sell properties to pay off the debt owed to Sir Dorabji. According to JRD, after selling the properties, all he had left was 'a stipend and the shares in Tata Sons'.[37] Despite this, JRD felt it was unfair that he was given all of the shares, so he divided them out among his siblings, Rodabeh, Jimmy, Sylla and Darab.

This act of generosity would have major significance in the years to follow. The siblings grew apart and fell out with JRD. Rodabeh and Darab sold the shares they had been given by JRD to Pallonji Mistry, heir to his family's massive construction company, the Shapoorji Pallonji Group (SP Group), of which he is today chairman.

If ever there was a situation of no good deed ever going unrewarded, this was definitely it.

It was his son, Cyrus Mistry, who succeeded Pallonji as a director on the Tata Sons board when he stepped down in 2006. Mistry was eventually selected to replace Ratan Tata as vice-chairman of Tata Sons in November 2011, with the remit that he would work alongside Ratan for one year and then replace him and take over as chairman. Twelve months later, Mistry did in fact take over as chairman of Tata Sons. He was removed by the board as chairman in October 2016 and replaced by Ratan Tata on an interim basis until a replacement was found.

This book is an attempt to explain how Cyrus Mistry became chairman and why Ratan and the board of Tata Sons later felt he had to be replaced.

The Mistry Family

It was 1865 when Pallonji Mistry's grandfather started a construction business in Mumbai in partnership with an Englishman. The initial project was Mumbai's first reservoir, near Malabar Hill. Over the years, the partners built automobile factories and steel mills for the Tata family.

Like the Tatas, the Mistrys are Zoroastrian Parsis. And like the Tatas, they too were blessed with a talent for business. The construction company grew through the years by landing major construction projects, which included such Mumbai landmarks as the Reserve Bank of India, the tower wing of the Taj Mahal Palace Hotel and Towers and the Oberoi Hotel. Pallonji Mistry started working for his father when he was only eighteen, and he rose to lead the company's expansion into the Middle East, with projects in Abu Dhabi, Qatar and Dubai during the 1970s. The firm crowned its reputation in the Middle East by building a palace complex for the Sultan of Oman.

During the same time frame, the Tata family business portfolio also grew exponentially, to well over 100 companies, among them the likes of Jaguar Land Rover (JLR), Tetley Tea and Corus Steel. In recent Indian newspaper reports, Pallonji Mistry is frequently referred to as 'the Phantom of Bombay House', in reference both to the name of Tata's corporate headquarters in Mumbai and the nearly silent demeanour of its largest individual shareholder.

Pallonji met and married Dublin-born Patsy Perin Dubash. They had four children, Shapoor, Cyrus, Laila and Aloo. Patsy and all four children have Irish passports and are Irish citizens. Years later, Pallonji himself took on Irish citizenship.

~

The new enterprises Dorabji and Ratanji founded were intended to bring India on par with the rest of the industrially developed world. This, of course, had been among Jamsetji's objectives as well. Dorabji went even further, looking beyond achieving mere equality with the industrial West. He wanted the Tata enterprises to achieve world-class status, and he became an enthusiastic promoter of the aviation initiatives of J.R.D. Tata in a bid to elevate India's image in the world.

In recognition of all he was achieving, Dorabji was knighted as part of the New Year's Honours list in 1910. It was an acknowledgement of the devotion and courage with which, in furthering his father's projects, he had also served the country. The knighthood was also something his father had not achieved and which thus signified official recognition of the work he did as a great industrialist in his own right.

To be sure, Dorabji faced critical challenges during his tenure as chairman. He took advantage of the post–World War I economic expansion to drive the extraordinary growth of Tata in the first quarter of the 20th century. In 1924, however, the company's upward trajectory flew through a perfect storm of economic reversals. The year saw, throughout the West, manufacturing costs generally spike in response to the salary demands of labour and sharp increases in the cost of transportation.

Since Tata was just then extending its own global reach, these increases hit the company hard. With rising costs came steep declines in revenue. As if this economic earthquake were not sufficient, an actual—and massive—earthquake hit Japan, instantly driving down the nation's demand for pig iron. Japan was Tata Steel's largest customer. It is possible that Dorabji did not realize the full dimension of the twin catastrophes—at least not until a telegram arrived from Jamshedpur informing the chairman that Tata Steel did not have enough money on hand to pay its employees. Dorabji responded by pledging to make up the shortfall from a loan against his personal wealth and using his wife's jewels as collateral. This would allow the company to continue operating. Dorabji's willingness to pierce the corporate veil and take a very personal risk proved critical to the survival of Tata Steel. It allowed the company to weather the storm and go on to renewed growth. The rising revenue was ploughed back into expanded production and the loan was repaid.

Dorabji suffered a fatal heart attack on 3 June 1932, having, along with Ratanji, faithfully fulfilled his father's dying wish.

～

Lady Navajbai Tata was far more than the bereaved widow of Sir Ratanji Tata. After her husband's death, she became the chairperson of the Sir Ratanji Tata Trust—first of the great Tata Trusts. She administered the trust with great skill. The generous donation made under her direction to the National Metallurgical Research Institute in Jamshedpur, for example, revealed her to be extraordinarily progressive in her management of philanthropic funds for innovative and constructive purposes.

In 1928, she was instrumental in creating the Sir Ratan Tata Institute, which was dedicated to reforming the manner of charitable giving to maximize the effect and sustainability of aid. The institute was designed to discourage the traditional charitable 'doles' and instead provide remunerative employment to the poor and, in particular, poor women by furnishing training and then employment opportunities.

None of Navajbai's philanthropic decisions were based on the consideration of caste or religion, and she did not hesitate to seek outside expertise to help her to craft wise decisions. As the Sir Ratanji Tata Trust chairperson, she invited S.J.I. Markham of the Carnegie Trust to study and report on problems within the Parsi community. The result of this report was a major reorganization of organized Parsi giving, to make sure the Parsi charities were self-supporting and therefore sustainable.

Finally, Lady Navajbai did not confine her charitable activities to administration. She lived the Parsi philosophy of giving. She owned a manor house called 'Homestead', at Matheran, a scenic hill station in the Western Ghats, a mountain retreat celebrated for its healthful air and popular as a weekend getaway from Mumbai and Pune. When a social worker approached her to allow Homestead to be used as a convalescent home, Lady Navajbai not only enthusiastically agreed and presented the property as a gift for this use, she also contributed Rs 2.5 lakh towards necessary renovation and construction work to make the conversion from manor to convalescent facility.

Lady Navajbai Tata would have been an honoured and memorable figure on the basis of her service as chairperson of the Sir Ratanji Tata Trust and on the Tata Sons board of directors, to which she was appointed (the first woman so honoured) in 1924—a position she held until her death in 1965. Her most profound contribution to the history and future of the Tata enterprise was, however, a family matter.

On 30 August 1904, a son was born in the extended Tata family headed by Hormusji Tata, who was married to Ratanbai Rao, the niece of Jamsetji Tata and his wife, Hirabai Daboo. (Ratanbai was the child of Hirabai's sister Cooverji Daboo, who had married Shapoorji Rao.) The child in question—the middle of five born to Hormusji and Ratanbai—was named Naval Hormusji Tata, after his father, Hormusji, a spinning master at Advanced Mills, a textile operation at Ahmedabad.[38]

In 1908, when Naval was just four, Hormusji Tata died suddenly, leaving Ratanbai and her five sons in straitened circumstances. She moved to Navsari, where she did embroidery to supplement a slim income. Unable to support her five children, she committed them to the care of the J.N. Petit Parsi Orphanage in Surat, a large port city on the coast of the state of Gujarat. Family friends contributed to give the children boarder status in the orphanage. As was the custom among Parsis earlier in the 20th century, if the head of the household died without a male heir, an heir would be chosen from within the extended family.

Accordingly, in 1919, encouraged by her brother-in-law, Sir Dorabji, Lady Navajbai decided to adopt one of Hormusji's five sons. Perhaps nothing more than chance prompted Lady Navajbai to choose instead the *middle* brother among the five, but colourful legend has it that her choice of Naval over the four others was based solely on what she saw as the beauty of his brown eyes. I asked Ratan if Lady Navajbai's unconventional choice created conflict between Naval and his brothers. 'No,' he answered. His father 'made sure they were looked after', providing financial assistance for all four of them and employment at Tata for two.[39]

Naval's birth mother had five sons. After the adoption of Naval by Lady Navajbai, as part of the adoption arrangement, Ratanbai moved into an apartment in Marine Drive in Mumbai, along with

Naval's four brothers, Jamasph, Shapoor, Shabak and Behram. This allowed Naval to see his biological mother and brothers. Jamasph and Shapoor each had a son, both of whom went to college in the United States. Jamasph's son, Hormuz (Homi for short), graduated from the Denver School of Mines and spent his entire career at US Steel, retiring in, I understand, a senior position in the research area of the company. Shapoor's son, Adi, graduated from a southern US university in textile engineering and worked in a large American textile company. As the US textile industry shrank, Adi started a small limousine company in New York City. Homi had four or more children who in turn have generated a number of grandchildren. Adi, who is also married, has no offspring.

Naval was already thirteen when Lady Navajbai selected him from the orphanage and planted him in the palatial Tata House. More important, thanks to Lady Navajbai's care and large fortune, Naval enjoyed good schooling and even enrolled in the University of Bombay (now University of Mumbai), where he earned a degree in economics. From here, he went to London, where he took up an accountancy course. He joined Tata Sons in 1930 as a clerk, soon getting promoted to the position of assistant secretary of Tata Sons and, in 1933, to secretary of its aviation department.

Naval's promotion to secretary of the aviation department came a year after Sir Dorabji Tata died, leaving, as Sir Ratanji had done in 1918, close to a 40 per cent stake in Tata Sons to a charitable trust—in Dorabji's case, the Sir Dorabji Tata Trust. As of 1942, the two trusts, the Sir Ratan Trust and the Sir Dorabji Trust, held just under 72 per cent of Tata Sons.

~

With the passing of Sir Dorabji, a person without the Tata name became the third chairman of the Tata Group. Nowroji Saklatwala was the son of Jamsetji's sister and a cousin of Dorabji. When he assumed the chairmanship, he faced an incredibly daunting challenge. The worldwide Great Depression that engulfed the 1930s demanded skilful consolidation of the conglomerate. Nowroji's character, a product of his upbringing, together with an intense involvement in the game of cricket, gave him the grit and the mental agility to lead the Tata enterprise through a most difficult era. Most impressively, his six-year chairmanship was not just a period of survival. It was a time of both social and financial progress for the company.

Nowroji was born in 1875 to Bapuji and Virbaiji Saklatwala (née Tata). Like his first cousin Dorabji, he was enrolled at St Xavier's College in Bombay. After graduation, he joined the Tata Group in 1899 as a clerk at Svadeshi Mills, at a monthly salary of Rs 50. What became quickly apparent to his supervisors was the agility of his mind. He was a quick study, and he was a very hard worker. He made himself master of the technical aspects of creating cotton products and soon acquired a confident grasp of the complex economics of the industry. Within a short time, he was promoted to leadership of the Tata textile mills.

Nowroji was a man of unflagging energy. Even after he became a member of management, despite a long workday, he would always be ready for an invitation to play a game of cricket. He credited the sport with keeping him fit as well as giving him the opportunity to develop and refine his leadership skills in the context of collaborative work. As a member of a team, he understood the importance of morale—and the necessity of compromising, at least sometimes. Indeed, his career as a Tata leader rose in tandem with his reputation as a cricketer. He was playing first-class cricket for the Parsi team of 1904–05 and was chosen to represent them against the Europeans. All good things, however, come to an end, and after a few years, the accumulation of professional responsibilities at Tata finally prevented him from continuing as a team member—though he never lost his enthusiasm for the game.

In 1917, the Bombay Mill Owners' Association named Nowroji its chairman, which was a measure of the respect and trust he enjoyed across the industry. Four years after this honour, he was chosen to represent Indian employers at the Third International Labour Conference in Geneva, much of which focused on progressive health and welfare issues. Increasingly, Nowroji became a force within the global textile industry. He received many offers to serve as adviser and honorary adviser to various committees, and he virtually never refused. His colleagues marvelled at his inexhaustible energy and commitment. With the outbreak of the Great War—World War I—Nowroji became a member of numerous war-related industrial committees and took on very real work as honorary adviser to the Munitions Board at the end of the war, during 1919–21.

Inside Tata, Nowroji was revered as both an adviser and a team player. He was a leader without an ego, always putting his colleagues and employees before himself. He was most comfortable working behind the scenes, in the background, quietly contributing guidance, counsel and leadership. Yet, when necessary, Nowroji spoke his mind frankly and even boldly. This was a reflection of his natural gifts as a leader who combined humility, respect and flexibility with a willingness to make and implement hard leadership decisions. Calm authority was what Nowroji projected, and it was a quality that drew him even further into the Tata inner circle. He soon worked alongside Dorabji Tata himself. This grew into a close and highly successful working relationship. Even though his name was not Tata, it came as no surprise that he was approached to succeed Dorabji as chairman in 1932.

The single most important formative element of the Nowroji leadership style was his experience of climbing up the worker ranks

in Tata Mills. He developed a profound fellow feeling for the
men on the factory floor and, as he ascended through the levels of
leadership, he incessantly advocated for employee benefits, which
was essentially unheard of during the early 20th century.

The sharing of profits was among these benefits. 'For some
time,' Nowroji remarked, 'we have been thinking about a method
of associating the employees of the company more definitely with
its prosperity in good times . . . You will be glad to hear that the
board shares our views that we ought to show our employees our
appreciation of their work when the company can afford to do so.
Will you give full publicity to this [profit-sharing scheme] among
all employees and let them know that it is the sincere wish of the
company as a whole that its employees should share properly in
its prosperity.'[40]

Within Tata, Nowroji became a crusader for labour reform.
In 1937—with India and most of the world still in the grip of
the Great Depression—he introduced higher wages for Tata's
lowest-paid workers. He also significantly improved working
conditions for temporary contractors hired by Tata Steel. Later,
he authorized a club as well as recreation rooms for employees at
Bombay House, Tata's corporate headquarters. He believed it was
critical to workers' health and morale that they should have a place
to enjoy fitness activities and simply relax.

What is most impressive about these accomplishments is that
Nowroji carried out his reforms during the worst global depression
in modern history. It was a time in which workers were willing to
be wage slaves, to complain about nothing and to accept what little
was given to them. In the spirit of the founders, Nowroji refused
to use economic conditions as an excuse to exploit his employees.

Nevertheless, cost-cutting and consolidation were urgent
imperatives during this period. Ways had to be found to do
more with less—but without taking it out on the workers.
Nowroji approached the problem as an issue of business strategy.

He concentrated the company on its core businesses, which were iron and steel, textile mills, banking and power. Cement was not a Tata business, let alone a core business, but Nowroji saw an opportunity to help several troubled Indian cement businesses through consolidation. It made business sense because, although Tata was not specifically in the cement business, it was involved in a very big way in Indian growth and construction. Cement, of course, was vital to these activities and therefore the acquisition and consolidation of cement companies was, in effect, a vertical expansion.

The venture into the cement industry began when the esteemed Bombay attorney, businessman and financier Framroze Edulji Dinshaw, the second son of the pre-eminent landowner and philanthropist of Karachi, Seth Edulji Dinshaw, proposed merging ten major cement companies into a single mega-firm. J.R.D. Tata later called Dinshaw 'the most brilliant man' he had ever met. So when Dinshaw presented his plan to Nowroji, the Tata chairman saw a great opportunity—one that not just meant profit, but, in the turbulent economic environment of the global depression, survival.

Dinshaw proposed merging the ten firms under Tata and the Khatau Group of Companies (an Indian conglomerate founded in 1874 and active in textiles, chemicals, shipping, aviation, automobiles and cement, before separating into its component companies in 1994) along with two other firms, Killick and Nixon, in addition to his own company. Unfortunately, Dinshaw died in 1938, leaving the incredibly complex merger incomplete. Like a fireman, Nowroji rushed in to broker the final deal. His approach was typically non-egocentric. His first step was to analyse and identify ten companies' common interests. With these established, it was clear that all had a stake in the success of the merger, and he was able to negotiate through their remaining differences in the context of their common good. The result was a solution that worked for all parties, and the new business, Associated Cement Companies Limited, was the very foundation of India's cement industry. Nowroji looked upon it with great and justifiable pride.

Like the two chairmen who preceded him, and like Lady Navajbai, Nowroji Saklatwala was a philanthropist. This was reflected first and foremost in his advocacy for Tata workers and for labour generally. As chairman of the Sir Dorabji Tata Trust, he directed funds towards the establishment of a specialist cancer hospital, the very first in India. On another note, he never forgot the sport that had meant so much to him. He devoted considerable energy to righting the imperilled ship that was the finances of the Cricket Club of India. His success in this endeavour was significant, and he served the club as its first chairman from its inception in 1933 until his death. He was instrumental in funding and developing Brabourne Stadium in Churchgate, Mumbai. A major sports venue, it was the very first permanent stadium in India.

Like other Tata chairmen, Nowroji received many honours for his years of public service. In 1917, he was made Justice of the Peace, and in 1923 was awarded the Order of the Indian Empire. A knighthood followed in 1933. He was made a Knight Commander of the Order of the British Empire in 1937. The following year, he succumbed to a massive heart attack while on a trip to France. He was succeeded as chairman by J.R.D. Tata, who would be, prior to Ratan Tata, the most iconic chairman of the Tata enterprise. This, along with the sheer longevity of JRD's chairmanship, which topped a half-century, overshadowed Nowroji's chairmanship, making it seem almost like a mere interregnum. It was no such thing. Thanks in no small measure to Nowroji Saklatwala's leadership in consolidating the Tata Group during the 1930s, the firm weathered the global economic depression.

2

Ratan Tata: The First Years

---

*In school, in college . . . Campion, Cathedral, Cornell and, later,
the Harvard Business School—each one of them was terrible when
you were there, questionable when you got out and later became
something that you really cherished and considered worthwhile.*

—Ratan Tata

Ratan Naval Tata was born to Naval and his first wife, Soonoo
Commissariat, on 28 December 1937, just before the Nowroji
chairmanship ended. His parents' marriage had been arranged,
as was traditional among Parsis, but had failed to develop into
a warm and loving relationship. The couple separated sometime
in the 1940s, when Ratan was still very young. Undeniably, then,
the family that Ratan's parents created, like the family into which
his father had been born, was somewhat dysfunctional, even by
modern standards. Yet, when asked about his childhood, Ratan
unhesitatingly declared that he had 'very happy memories'.[1] Given
that the family's history was marked by early death and marital
discord, this response is rather unexpected.[2]

Naval, Soonoo, Ratan and Jimmy (Ratan's brother) had
all lived in Tata House with Lady Navajbai. Soonoo left Tata

House when she parted ways with his father, eventually marrying the man she had loved all along and had wanted, from the very beginning, to marry.[3] This man was none other than Sir Jamsetjee Jejeebhoy, 6th Baronet of Bombay and among the most famous Parsis in India.

Ratan noted that, for Lady Navajbai, Sir Jamsetjee's fame was like salt in the wound, following what she felt was a desertion by Soonoo. As for Ratan, he says that Sir Jamsetjee was always very generous and polite to both Jimmy and him. He always made them feel welcome when they visited. And Soonoo had had a positive impact on Sir Jamsetjee, Ratan observed. Before marrying her, he had been something of a playboy. He did not really have a job and instead passed his time playing polo and golf. Soonoo quickly put him to work and pushed him to get involved with boards of companies and in other productive pursuits.

Lady Navajbai Tata was certainly not pleased to have Naval and Soonoo divorced, with two young sons, but she remained dignified and supportive of retaining the family integrity. She supported Ratan's and Jimmy's visits to Soonoo and always spoke in friendly terms about Soonoo. Lady Navajbai took it upon herself to be a surrogate mother to Ratan and Jimmy and did a superb job of filling the void as best as she could in those early years. For Soonoo, her marriage and her children were her duty, but Lady Navajbai never forgave Soonoo for the divorce. Without question, however, she fell in love with the couple's children and, following Soonoo's departure, embraced both Ratan and his younger brother, Jimmy, as her own, raising them in Tata House. She would prove to be the single-most important influence on Ratan during his early years, greater even than his father or birth mother.

While Lady Navajbai was a most formidable 'maternal' presence in Ratan's early life, her influence on him was, on balance, overwhelmingly positive, and his feelings for her remain deep. So calling his family 'somewhat dysfunctional' should not be interpreted as painting Ratan as a 'poor little rich boy'. Far from it. He certainly was not abused, and he certainly was blessed in that he never had to worry about where his next meal would come from. In a physical, economic and cultural sense, his was in fact a very comfortable upbringing. Although sheltered, and even insulated, Ratan's early life also included a very fine education. Yet everything about his upbringing was defined and even circumscribed by the understanding instilled in him of what it meant to be a Tata. In terms of the socially conscious, patriotic and philanthropic business legacy that Jamsetji Tata and his sons, Sir Ratanji and Sir Dorabji, created, it was a glorious legacy. Still, it was not necessarily an easy burden to carry. As a result, Ratan's childhood, in the free and joyful sense, typically associated with childhood, did not really begin until he went to America as a young man.

Naval remarried in 1955. His second wife was Simone Dunoyer, a Swiss woman born and raised in Geneva and a graduate of Geneva University, who rose, by 1962, to a board position within the Tata Group. She revived a small Tata company, Lakme, transforming it into a leading cosmetics company in India, with large export sales and a national image. Ratan developed a cordial relationship with her, and many years later, while he was chairman of Tata Sons, supported her plans for creating a genuine retail enterprise in Trent Ltd,[4] of which she became the non-executive chairman.

Although Naval remained very much in Ratan's early life, at least until he remarried, young Ratan was largely raised by his grandmother, Lady Navajbai. He still had a respectful, though not particularly close, father–son relationship with Naval. But when asked about his father, he implies that such respectful distance between fathers and sons was not uncommon when he was coming of age.

In good Parsi fashion, Naval was eloquent on the subject of his own, more intense, childhood struggles: 'I am grateful to God for giving me an opportunity to experience the pangs of poverty, which more than anything [else] moulded my character in the later years of my life.'[5]

Naval's son by his second wife, Simone, Noel Tata, provides a revealing insight into his father's character. He rose through the ranks of Tata Sons and achieved prominence, positioning Noel to rise to the chairmanship of Trent Ltd., the Tata Group's retail arm, and to become the managing director of Tata International as well as chairman of Tata Investment Corporation. Noel told me that Naval never forgot his humble beginnings.[6]

Noel, who is twenty years younger than Ratan and has a substantial physical resemblance to him, is quite different in demeanour. Where Ratan is naturally reserved, Noel is more outwardly emotional. When asked about his father, it becomes immediately apparent that he had a very different relationship with Naval as compared to Ratan. For example, he always referred to Naval as 'Daddy', whereas to Ratan he was always 'my father'. Noel was also effusive about his father's warmth: 'Everyone liked Daddy.' Noel had a much closer relationship with Naval than Ratan had, while Ratan had a much warmer, closer relationship with JRD.

When Noel was asked if he felt Naval would have approved of Cyrus being fired, his response was that he did not think his dad would have agreed to an 18.4 per cent shareholder being appointed in the first place, but that he would have certainly supported the separation. And when asked if he had been surprised to hear of Cyrus's firing, he said, 'Whilst many in the business community and indeed many in India were surprised, some of the senior leadership within the Tata Group were aware that the tensions had been growing and that it was only a matter of time before matters came to a head.'

Naval Tata: The Unsung Protector of the Flame

Naval Tata rose from an entry-level position in Tata Sons as a clerk in 1930, was promoted to assistant secretary of Tata Sons and then to secretary of the aviation department. In person and in photographs, Ratan often smiles. It is a warm, spontaneous smile, which clearly comes naturally to him. Photographs of Naval, in contrast, reveal a handsome man who certainly resembles his son, but who neither smiles nor frowns. His is the face of a professional, a businessman and, above all, a stoic.

In 1938, Naval earned an executive position in the textiles department and, the following year, was appointed joint managing director of Tata Mills, the central company that ran all the textile mills of Tata. He was appointed managing director in 1947—the equivalent of CEO at the time—of Tata Mills and also became managing director of Tata Oil Mills Co. Ltd the following year. He served as chairman of the Ahmedabad Advance Mills in Ahmedabad. He was a director of Tata Sons and rose to become deputy chairman of the holding company. Ultimately, he had direct management responsibility for the three Tata electric companies, the four Tata textile mills and the chairmanship of the Sir Ratanji Tata Trust.

Beyond his management of the trust, Naval was very active in a number of other philanthropic organizations, doing social, educational and welfare work. In 1951, he co-founded the Indian Cancer Society, the first such organization in the country, and served as a trustee of a number of non-Tata trusts. In the spirit and tradition of what has been called the Tatas' 'compassionate capitalism', Naval had a special interest in bridging the gap between management and labour. This led him to intensive study and activism in the field, and he became an internationally recognized authority on labour relations. He served as a member of the governing body of the International Labour Organization and was elected to that body thirteen times—a record that remains unbroken to this day. He wrote or co-wrote a series of authoritative reports, including *In Pursuit of Industrial Harmony: An Employer's Perspective* (1976), *A Policy for Harmonious Industrial Relations* (1980) and *On Wage Problem and Industrial Unrest.*

~

Naval was clearly concerned about properly preparing his firstborn for a career in the family business and so continued to be a presence in Ratan's life. Ratan had great respect for his father. The fact that Naval provided for the four brothers Lady Navajbai did not adopt earned Ratan's deep respect, if not the unfettered fullness of his love. There developed a kind of symmetry in the family. Jimmy was closer to his father than Ratan, while Ratan was much closer to Lady Navajbai than Jimmy.

The relationship between Naval and his first wife, Soonoo, became less tense—although still cool, at best—and Noel's birth in 1957 eased tensions further. Perhaps the discontent of his parents' union and the bitterness of their eventual separation hit Jimmy harder than it did Ratan. Being older than Jimmy, Ratan may well have possessed a fuller understanding of the ways of the heart as well as the dynamics of the marriage and the divorce. Without question, however, Ratan and Jimmy were very close as children, and Jimmy looked up to his older brother. Ratan and Jimmy would visit their mother, although since neither his father nor Lady Navajbai approved of such visits, they were few and far between. Ratan did take pleasure in the fact that Soonoo's second marriage gave Jimmy and him three half-sisters: Shireen, born in 1952; Deanna, born in 1953; and Geeta, born in 1955. At one point, while his mother was refurbishing her home, she and the three girls lived with Ratan in his apartment. It was crowded, Ratan recalls, but he did not at all mind them being there. Sadly, one of the sisters, Geeta has since passed away, but the other two live in Mumbai, and Ratan remains close to them.

As for Ratan's love for his mother and loyalty to her, there was never any doubt. Young Ratan studied in America at Cornell University, earning degrees in engineering and architecture. He used his architectural education to design only two houses: his own beach house off the Arabian Sea and his mother's house in Mumbai.[7] Perhaps an even greater testament of his feelings for his birth mother came in 1981–82, when Soonoo was diagnosed with cancer. Ratan flew with her to New York City to the Sloan Kettering Institute. He carved out four months to be with her throughout the complete course of treatment.[8]

~

Ratan received his earliest sustained experience of the world beyond the Tatas when his grandmother enrolled him at Campion School. Established in 1943 by a Jesuit priest, Father Joseph Savall, Campion was—and is—a day school located on Cooperage Road, across the street from Mumbai's principal soccer stadium, Cooperage Ground. Despite its proximity to a sports stadium, Ratan recalls having little interest in sports in school. 'I don't remember too much about sports [in school],' he says. 'I remember that my grandmother used to have this huge antiquated Rolls-Royce and she used to send that car to pick my brother and me up from school. Both of us used to be so ashamed of that car that we used to walk back home. That is the sport that I remember.'[9] Indeed, after a time, he arranged for Lady Navajbai's chauffeur to drop him off some distance from the school, lest his classmates think he was spoilt.

Like most children, Ratan was eager to fit in. And like most children, he wasn't always thrilled about studying. 'The Parsi community is very particular about good education,' Ratan told an interviewer for *Daily News & Analysis* in 2010. As if going to a demanding school were not hard enough work, Ratan recalls,

'Most of us were forced to have tuitions [small-group tutoring sessions] whether you wanted it or not after school. Life was quite a drudgery in those days.' But when he was pressed to give advice to students of today, Ratan emphasized that the 'most important thing that you look back on is the quality of education that you were given', and he implied that a reliable measure of that quality is the degree of drudgery you felt when that education was being administered to you. 'In school, in college . . . Campion, Cathedral, Cornell and, later, the Harvard Business School (HBS)—each one of them was terrible when you were there, questionable when you got out, and later became something that you really cherished and considered worthwhile.'[10]

At Campion, he 'liked physics a lot' but not chemistry, perhaps because physics invites you to ask the very biggest questions, whereas chemistry is more limited in scope.[11] Physics reaches beyond the intellect to touch the imagination. When Ratan was in the 9th standard, Campion School could not afford to build the additional facilities required, and all the students in the 9th standard were obliged to transfer to other schools. Ratan transferred to the Cathedral and John Connon School, another high-end Mumbai day school. Where Campion was ranked second throughout India, Cathedral was ranked first. While the motto of Campion was *Gaudium in Veritate* ('Joy in Truth'), that of Cathedral was *Clarum Efficiunt Studia* ('Studies Maketh Famous'). Campion was established in 1943. Cathedral was much more venerable, having been founded in 1860, and it had—and has today—a reputation as a training academy for the children of India's richest and most elite families, especially those families associated with Indian business. Numerous Tatas and Mistrys attended, including Cyrus, but so did the likes of Bollywood actress Amisha Patel; diplomat Arundhati Ghose; supermodel Ashwin Shetty; internationally distinguished journalist Fareed Zakaria; Booker Prize-winning author Kiran Desai; founder of Pakistan Muhammad, Ali Jinnah; and another Booker Prize winner, the controversial novelist Salman Rushdie.[12]

At Cathedral, Ratan was in rarefied company, yet he recalls, 'None of us was flamboyant in those days and it didn't matter whether you were rich or poor. There was a terrific amount of camaraderie.' He considered this democratic fellow-feeling the single greatest value conveyed by his education, since he commented that, 'unfortunately, we tend to disengage from [such equalizing camaraderie] when we walk out of school or walk out of college'. It is, he said, something we should 'try to preserve'.[13] In 2009, he addressed Cathedral alumni and spoke of his 'dream India', a place 'where every Indian has an equal opportunity to shine on merit. In a country like ours, you have to try to live and lead by example, not flaunt your wealth and prominence.'[14] Indeed, in a 2011 interview published in *The Times of India*, Ratan expressed dismay and surprise at the lavish lifestyle of some of the senior members of the business community. He was concerned about the lack of empathy for the poor.

Ratan lives in what is usually described as a 'modest house in Mumbai', which it is.[15] Despite the camaraderie he felt in school, Ratan confessed to being shy. 'One thing I have never recovered from is a fear of public speaking. The only people speaking publicly in school were those reading out the sermon at assembly and those participating in debates. I wasn't among either. Nor was I into too many extra-curricular activities. In that, I missed the full culture of Cathedral and it's my loss.' Indeed, there were times when Ratan doubted he would survive to graduate. 'Cathedral for me was a mixed bag. I particularly remember a mathematics teacher who, I felt, was determined that I never complete school. He almost succeeded.'[16]

Ratan Tata's childhood, while very far from being sad, was also seriously disrupted by his parents' marital discord and divorce. Things like these happen in all families—but the Tatas are both a family and a family business, an enormous family business of great consequence to India and to employees, partners, investors and other stakeholders all over the world. For this reason, the Tatas have handled such commonly occurring disruptions differently than other families.

Indian business historian Gita Piramal says that she has argued with Ratan over her perception that he was 'never . . . fully reconciled to being the scion of a family firm.' She implies that the reason for what she sees as Ratan's ambivalence is that the 'Tatas are a reconstructed family who adopt and cobble together people to make a family. That way they do promote talent rather than blood relations. Ratan was clearly talented, but he resents the implication.'[17]

Nevertheless, Piramal's choice of words, 'cobble together', is glib. Clearly, the family members who were or are also leaders of the family business have always recognized that the Tata Group is bigger not only than any individual but also than any single family. For this reason, they have always been willing to give nature a helping hand. As Randeep Ramesh put it in a 2008 article for *The Guardian*, 'In many ways Ratan Tata is an accidental millionaire, a gifted interloper in a family that had everything but children . . . The Tatas slowly built up a formidable business but by 1917 the family was running out of heirs . . .'[18]

What the Tatas did possess in abundance, however, was rootedness in India's Parsi community. It is a small and ethnic group—69,000 as of 2006 and declining[19]—concentrated in and around Mumbai, as well as in Bangalore, Pune and Hyderabad, in addition to Karachi, Pakistan. Today's Parsis—their name means 'Persians'—are descended from refugees who fled Persia (modern Iran) during the 8th through 10th centuries, the period of the Arab conquest of their country. The Zoroastrianism they practise is a very ancient faith, which history first records in the 5th century BC, predating both Christianity and Islam, and has as its 'basic doctrine . . . a universal ethical precept: 'Good thoughts, good words, good deeds''.[20]

The moral and spiritual duty of a Zoroastrian may be stated quite straightforwardly: it is to do the right thing because it *is* the right thing, and to live life such that what you say and what you do make the lives of others better. This compact constellation of values is held by the Parsi community in India that has also developed a rich culture of business and trade.[21]

In contrast to the West, where religious values often clash with or are assumed to be incompatible with competitive capitalism, among the Indian Parsis, doing business is not only compatible with ethical and philanthropic action, it is essential to it. The objective of a successful business is to do well by doing good. For the Parsis, making a profit is not a zero-sum game; winning does not require making someone else a loser. On the contrary, a good business makes money *and* makes the lives of others in the community better.

The Tata family as a business family is a combination of genetics, strategic marriage, adoption and mentoring. It is very likely that Ratan's rise to leadership benefitted from the willingness of the Tatas to 'cobble together', from wherever in the extended family they found it, the talent needed to grow and prosper the family business. Ratan paid and sacrificed a lot for his inheritance. Yes, there were many benefits but, overall, his commitment to the Tata Legacy deprived him of the joys of parenthood. If Ratan had married and had five or six children, would he have been able to devote himself to the mission that was an integral part of his DNA? It was nothing less than a part of his childhood or, at least, certain aspects of it. Yet his character evolved away from the dominating influence of his father and others, while remaining open to the religious and ethical values the Tatas shared with India's small but remarkably influential Parsi community. These values are perhaps his family's greatest gift to him.

3

From the Factory Floor

Do it because you have a passion for it. You have to have the passion to make a success of what you do.

—Ratan Tata

Naval Tata was the longest-serving Tata Sons board member, and spent much of his time on the board as a close associate of the longest-serving chairman of Tata Sons, J.R.D. Tata, Ratan's immediate predecessor. The lines of familial and business relationships crossed and, quite likely, put some emotional strain on Ratan's relationship with his father. Without a doubt, Naval had a most distinguished career at Tata, but it was JRD—dashing, Paris-born and exquisitely cosmopolitan—who emerged as the firm's truly charismatic and iconic business leader, earning a reputation that was not bound by the Indian subcontinent.

To the modest degree that it is even possible to separate Tata family relationships from Tata business relationships, Ratan, from a business perspective, grew much closer to JRD than to his own father. While Naval created conditions that helped prepare Ratan for a Tata career, he was never truly a mentor to the young man.

JRD, however, not only served as a mentor but was also Ratan's business role model and avid promoter.

It is not hyperbole to observe that, in significant ways, JRD was more of a father figure for Ratan than his actual father was. In any event, the admiration between JRD and Ratan was mutual and powerful. So, ironically, while it was Naval, an often remote and, for long stretches, more or less absent father, who prepared his son to play important roles in the family business, it was JRD who ultimately positioned him for a rapid rise to the top.

Ratan does not speak easily or at length about a childhood that was abridged or deferred, or even suspended, in his earliest years. Certainly, he was acutely aware that he was a member of a very special family. He speaks fondly about his relationship with his brother Jimmy and how they used to be very close; more recently, unfortunately, they have drifted apart. He has fond memories of times spent with Jimmy when the two were growing up.[1] However, after Ratan returned from Cornell and joined the business, they started to grow apart. There was no single incident that caused the rift, such as it was. But there may have been an element of jealousy, starting with the fact that Ratan was clearly Lady Navajbai's favourite and Jimmy was much closer to Naval. But when Noel was born in 1957—while Ratan was at college in the United States—it must have been hard for Jimmy. This seems to be a source of sadness for Ratan. It is apparent that he would like to mend bridges with Jimmy, but Jimmy has become such a recluse that he rarely leaves his home.

Noel can recall heated disputes between JRD and his father,[2] and confirms Ratan's story of how he—Ratan—was obliged to mediate and restore burnt bridges after JRD and Naval had one major argument or another. Noel also recalls many details of his father's commitment to workers' rights and how he had been voted on to the International Labour Organization (ILO) a record thirteen times.

Of his adoptive grandmother, Lady Navajbai, Noel had little to say. Strangely, he remembered her as 'meek', an adjective few, if any, have ever used to describe her. But the fact is that Noel was only seven years old when she died. He lived in Tata House until his twenty-seventh year. When asked if he got 'a chance to catch up with Ratan much these days', he replied, 'Not enough.'

~

Ratan regularly advises aspiring entrepreneurs: 'Do it because you have a passion for it. You have to have the passion to make a success of what you do.'[3] He lives by this advice today in his work as an entrepreneur and angel investor, but this is precisely the way he felt as a young man when he made a critical decision about the direction of his studies at Cornell University. Naval approved of his going there to study, but insisted that he study engineering, because a degree in that discipline would be useful in his career. This was perfectly reasonable preparation—but it was direct preparation for a functional, somewhat restrictive career at Tata, rather than a truly strategic leadership position. In contrast to Naval, JRD, as a mentor, would never constrain Ratan in this way.

Ratan's first extended experience beyond the Tata cocoon was his very first trip to the United States, when he was 'eleven years old or so'. He had come at the invitation of a United Nations official, a friend of his father's, who invited him to stay with the family on Long Island, New York. Years later, Ratan recalled, 'It was as though I had always been here. It was a strange thing. I had absolutely no sense of having to adapt.' This feeling 'reinforced a view that this is where I wanted to go to college'.[4]

He enrolled at Cornell University in 1955 as part of the class of 1959, intending to obey his father's wish to get a degree in engineering, but instead ended up staying on through 1962, so

that he could pursue a degree in architecture. It was his passion—
but not the path his father wanted for him. While in college,
Ratan regularly spent Thanksgiving or Easter vacation with two
more of his father's friends, Ed and Sylvia Vinnicombe. Ed had
graduated from the Cornell Hotel School, and he and his wife
became Ratan's 'surrogate parents'.

Ed Vinnicombe was vice-president of the McCormick spice
company in Baltimore, and it was at their Baltimore home, Ratan
recalls, that 'I learnt so much about how to wash dishes, how to
make my bed and all those things'. He also learnt to drive—cars
were always a Ratan Tata passion—and his first driver's licence
was from the state of Maryland.[5]

While an American college student, Ratan lived free of the
burden of being a Tata. The freedom that most of us experience in
the long span of childhood, he finally packed into a few youthful
years spent in America. He traded engineering for architecture,
and learnt to drive, to fly, and to bond with really bright people,
who knew nothing about the Tata legacy and therefore treated
him as an equal.

When asked what he liked most about America, Ratan replied,
'I think what I loved about America—and still do—is the fact that
it remains one of the places where if you had merit or capability,
you had a chance to make it happen. It may not be that everybody
with capability becomes a great success, but anybody willing to
work hard and to be diligent has a fair chance. The United States
has less of an issue of who you are, whose son you are, how rich
you are as a requirement for success. So, you can be successful
from the street, if you had the capability.'[6]

Ratan offered an example from his years at Cornell. 'There
used to be—I still remember him, a person called Chuck Feeney.
He was a student who started a business of distributing sandwiches
at ten at night. And he'd come with his sandwich basket, and the
College of Architecture was full of students at that time of night.

And the word would be out: *Chuck's here with sandwiches!* And we'd all go and buy his sandwiches—which were just great.'

The Chuck Feeney to whom he referred turned out to be a billionaire known best for giving his fortune away.

Charles Francis 'Chuck' Feeney was born in 1931 to Irish-American parents, in the gritty industrial town of Elizabeth, New Jersey. He co-founded in 1960 the Duty Free Shoppers Group, which made him a fortune. He then invested in General Atlantic Partners, a private equity firm, which turned into one of the best dotcom investors of all time. Twenty-two years later, in 1982, he founded the Atlantic Philanthropies, which focus on liberal public policy initiatives in Australia, Bermuda, South Africa, Vietnam, the United States and Ireland. Two years after establishing the organization, he secretly conveyed to it his entire stake in GAP Duty Free Shoppers: 38.75 per cent. Moreover, he managed to keep his philanthropy a secret until it was revealed in a 1997 business dispute. In 2011, he signed on to 'The Giving Pledge' initiated by Bill Gates and Warren Buffet, formally agreeing to do what he had been doing all along—donating most of his net worth to philanthropy. To date, this amounts to some $8 billion given away.

'And you know that it could only happen in the United States,' Ratan remarked of Feeney's rise from sandwich guy to billionaire, and his further rise to leading philanthropist. 'It was an example of an enterprising student who was fantastically successful. It makes one feel very proud.'

Ratan was raised in one of the most famous families of India, a family whose business interests evolved to become one of the largest philanthropic enterprises in the world. He gets away to America, enrols in a great American university, breaks with his father's wishes and studies architecture instead of engineering and meets a whole gallery of bright people, most of them fellow students, including an Irish-American who makes good money by making great sandwiches. This is how he meets Chuck Feeney, who goes on to build a fortune, only to do with it what the Tatas have been doing with theirs. He gives it away.

Only in America? Not quite. The Tatas and Chuck Feeney—and, for that matter, Bill Gates and Warren Buffett—all have life stories with one key plot element in common: unstinting philanthropy. No wonder Ratan felt at home in America. The Tata family values prepared him for it.

'Feeney is just the kind of, you know, his humility and his desire to remain anonymous wherever and whenever it is, is one side of the coin,' Ratan commented. 'The other side is the fact that he's so large-hearted and so successful. What I'm trying to say is the United States makes that possible.' In Chuck Feeney, Irish-American, Ratan Tata of India recognized a kindred spirit.

For Ratan, Feeney was the ideal example of philanthropy. When asked what he thought about the Buffett/Gates concept of getting rich people to pledge to give away their money, his response was surprising.[7] Ratan said, 'You cannot emotionally convince or coerce people into being generous and philanthropic. Either they are or they are not. If they want to give, they will give, if they do not, they will not, but putting social medial pressure on them, I do not think that is the right way to do it.' As for himself, he was so grateful for the time he spent at Cornell that, in 2008, the Tata Education and Development Trust gave a $50-million gift to the university, half of which was used to create the Tata-Cornell Institute for Agriculture and Nutrition (TCI), a long-term research initiative focusing on 'innovative interventions linking agriculture, food systems, human nutrition and poverty in India'.[8]

His experience at Cornell gave Ratan a glimpse of a unique model of entrepreneurship and philanthropy in Chuck Feeney. It gave him an opportunity to choose his own path of study. It also allowed him to nurture his early passion for automobiles and aircraft, both of which were forms of self-expression and liberation.

Ratan was in his late seventies when he remarked, 'You know my passion is cars, and my passion is also right now looking at what plane I can buy—or, rather, what helicopter I can buy that would give me freedom to go short distances. So, I've been looking at the Robinson.'[9]

Robinson Helicopter Company of Torrance, California, is a maker of three models of small corporate rotary-wing aircraft. Ratan, like JRD before him, is an enthusiastic fixed-wing pilot. Ratan who is a type-rated licensed pilot, often personally flies the company's Dassault Falcon 2000 business jet. But his interest in helicopters had apparently recently resurfaced, despite some prior harrowing flying experiences.

He tells the story of losing an engine while flying a helicopter in college:

'I lost an engine on a helicopter—a single-engine helicopter,' he responds calmly, 'and I'm still here . . .'

'And I was over water.'

'I made it just to the tip of the land.'

When asked if that was closest he had come to death, he replied, 'No, I actually didn't think it was close to death at all,' he answered like a true pilot, the kind who defines a 'good landing' as any you walk away from. 'I can't say I *lost* an engine. What I think happened was that water got into the fuel tank, and the engine quit but then it kind of like surged, and then I lost it again and it came alive again and surged. So, I was powering back the engine because I was concerned we were just going to go uncontrolled. And so I was able to make it to landfall, which I could see, and so I landed.'

But Ratan had not run out of flying stories.

'I've been in a plane twice where I lost an engine—a single-engine plane. So, I had to glide in.'

'The first time I was just doing circuits and landings, so that was easy. But the second time, I was with three classmates flying around Cornell and about 9 miles from the airport and made it back to the airport and landed.'

Fortunately for us, this near-catastrophe has been preserved for posterity in a video-recorded interview with Ratan and two of his passengers.[10] It tells a lot about the character of the man. Ratan's Cornell classmate Moises Benchoam begins:

> I remember that day, and we were in the drafting room working on our architectural project. And Ratan asked if anybody wanted to take a break and go fly with him. Charlie Green, Nan Otteson, and myself took his offer. And pretty soon, we were high above Cayuga's waters, enjoying beautiful scenery from a rented [Piper] Tri-Pacer single-engine plane.

> NANNETTE OTTESON: Mo [Moises] and I were in the rear seats, and Charlie was in the co-pilot position. When we got up over Sibley [Hall], Tata said, 'Oh, look at the dome.' There's Sibley's dome, where we all should have been.

> RATAN TATA: And the next moment, it seemed like the whole plane was shaking itself apart, and then the prop stopped, and I realized we had no engine. There was dead silence outside the plane. Inside the plane, too.

> MOISES BENCHOAM: I didn't know what was going on. I just saw Ratan moving levers and trying to control the plane. And when I leaned forward to see what was going on, I saw the propeller, that it was frozen.

> RATAN TATA: I decided that I would try to land on the first place I saw, which was the practice field next to the stadium. And then I realized that all these people were practising for the football game, and I'd come in and kill them all because

there was no sound. So, then I decided I'd try to make the airport.

MOISES BENCHOAM: And I remember Ratan turning back to us and saying that we were high enough to make a forced landing at the runway in the airport. I turned towards Nan, and I saw her sinking as far as she could into her seat. And I didn't get scared. I just wanted to see what Ratan was going to do.

NANETTE OTTESON: And then I heard him make the mayday call, and then I knew we were really in trouble. And then all of a sudden, I saw the tree-line coming up, and I looked over at Mo Benchoam, and he looked at me. We didn't say a word. Neither did Charlie Green. But I was sure we were going to end up in the trees. And then all of a sudden, we came down, and we were at the airport. It was a miracle.

RATAN TATA: And I made the airport—but the wrong side of the airport. And I know there's a Mohawk airlines plane coming in the other way, so I flicked on my landing lights and landed. He went around, and I made probably the best landing I've ever made, and rolled on to the taxiway, turned off the runway, and then got everybody to get out and push the plane. Because there was no engine. And we had this big Mohawk plane behind us, sort of bearing down on us, trying to get us out of the way— because he had to go around and come back.

MOISES BENCHOAM: Ratan asked the guy in the control tower why he hadn't answered his calls. And the guy said that he had gone out for a Coke. So, then he went to the guy he rented the airplane from, and he said that if he wanted his plane back, he had to get it at the end of the runway. And the guy just said, 'Well, that's better than fishing it out of Cayuga Lake.'

'For many years I had this piston with a hole in it sitting on my desk,' Ratan recalls. 'It was a treasured souvenir.'

Passenger Nan Otteson remarked, 'I was very grateful for Tata's calmness in the situation, and his skill in getting us all down. And I thanked him very much for this.'

~

Ratan was not anxious to give up the freedom he found in America, but he did want to get out of the cold, which he 'never did get used to', complaining that he 'couldn't ever feel warm enough'. Vowing that he 'would never live in a cold climate again', he left Ithaca as soon as his coursework was completed, but instead of returning to India, he headed out to Los Angeles, where he moved to an apartment complex, complete with swimming pool. He intended to use his architecture degree to get a job in the area and, eventually, to set up as an American architect. He had no intention of returning to India. However, his grandmother, Lady Navajbai, fell critically ill and called for him. He could not resist flying back to India to be with her. He had an American girlfriend at that time who was to follow him to India but never did. Lady Navajbai survived the crisis, but her health continued to deteriorate, and Ratan found himself extending his stay in India.

In later life, Ratan spoke of having four serious girlfriends in his life and 'once even got engaged, but broke it off before the cards could be printed'.[11] But he never married, and the absence of a spouse and children has, over the years, caused some to speculate about what motivates this incredibly motivated man. The bond he felt with Lady Navajbai was strong enough to pull him out of Los Angeles and back to India, and after a short period of time, he got drawn into working in the Tata organization. It was one of those emotionally driven decisions. As for avoiding marriage, it could well be that the example of his parents' unhappy union made him gun-shy.

What had moved Ratan to leave America and return to India to begin a career in the Tata organization? It was certainly not what he had trained for at Cornell. Nor, he once said, was it the money. 'Perhaps,' he offered, 'the challenge' was sufficient to have motivated his career. Yet, he mused, 'If I had an ideological choice, I would probably want to do something more for the uplift of the people of India. I have a strong desire not to make money but to see happiness created in a place where there isn't.'[12]

~

When Jamsetji Tata's nephew and Tata chairman Nowroji Saklatwala died in 1938, the chairmanship passed to Jehangir Ratanji Dadabhoy Tata—JRD—the son of Jamsetji's cousin. Born in Paris to Ratanji Dadabhoy Tata and his French wife, Suzanne Brière Tata, JRD received a cosmopolitan education in India, London, Japan and France. A French citizen, he served a year in the French Army and became passionate about flying—as Ratan was. In 1929, he earned the first pilot's licence issued in India and just three years later founded India's first commercial airline, Tata Airlines. (It would become Air India after World War II, and from 1986 to 1989, Ratan would serve as its chairman.)

Lady Navajbai's summoning of Ratan to return to India was soon followed by JRD's formal invitation to join the firm. In accepting, Ratan wrote that he would 'attempt to express my thanks by serving the firm as best as I can, and . . . do all I can to make sure that you will not regret your decision'.[13]

Ironically, more than sixty years later, this was likely one of the reasons he realized that allowing Cyrus to remain chairman of Tata Sons would be the wrong decision.

Ratan did not begin his Tata career in a corner office. In 1962, he was sent to work in Jamshedpur, in the factory of Tata Engineering and Locomotive Company—TELCO—and, after six months, was transferred to what was then called Tata Iron and Steel Company Limited (TISCO). Here he spent two years on the shop floor, shovelling limestone and tending the blast furnace, before moving up to the engineering division and, finally, to the position of technical assistant to TISCO'S CEO (at the time called the director-in-charge). Clearly, Ratan's bosses sent favourable reports to JRD, who called him to Bombay (today Mumbai), briefly sent him to Australia, and then recalled him once again to Bombay. In 1971, JRD gave him command (as director-in-charge) of what Ratan later characterized as 'two sick companies'. The assignments, he said, were made 'supposedly to train me'. One of the 'ailing' firms was NELCO, a radio and television manufacturer, and the other was Central India Textiles.[14]

Being assigned to lead the Central India Spinning Weaving and Manufacturing Company made sense, since Ratan's father, Naval, had long been involved with the firm's mills. Indeed, Ratan later commented, with justifiable pride, that under his leadership, 'Central India was turned around, its accumulated losses were wiped out and it paid dividends for some years'. A recession in the textile industry, however, later drove it into voluntary liquidation. No one blamed Ratan for the recession that laid Central India low, but NELCO was another story. Its history was troubled, and that 'has forever been held against me', Ratan later reflected.

When, in 1973, he was named director of Tata Industries, some outsiders, citing NELCO, complained that the promotion was undeserved and conferred only on account of his surname. In his own defence, Ratan has pointed out that NELCO actually became profitable and 'went from a 2 per cent market share to a 25 per cent share'. In fact, the company remained profitable under his leadership from 1972 to 1975, when the general recession crippled demand for consumer goods.[15]

Back to School

Ratan had already compiled a creditable management record when he felt the need to go back to school and learn more. Perhaps he was driven by the Parsi belief in education, the belief that if some education is good, more education is better. Perhaps, having had a taste of managing difficult companies in difficult times, he simply felt that he needed to know more. Whatever the motive, in 1975, he enrolled in the Advanced Management Program (AMP) at Harvard Business School (HBS).

HBS is best known for its prestigious MBA programme, of course, but business leadership insiders have long revered the intensive AMP and knew it to be precisely what Harvard advertises it as: 'a life-altering and career changing program' with 'a fully immersive format [that] will forever change the way you and your company do business'.[16] At the time Ratan enrolled, AMP was a thirteen-week programme. 'As I look back, those thirteen weeks were probably the most important thirteen weeks of my life. They transformed me and my perspective,' he told attendees at a December 2013 ceremony to dedicate Tata Hall. It is a gently curving seven-story, 161,000-square-foot building, with upper floors of sparkling limestone and glass that perch atop a three-story glass wall. According to William Rawn, the building's architect, this design was a response to Ratan's question to him, which he took as a charge: 'Can the building touch the ground lightly?'[17]

Tata Hall combines classroom and dormitory facilities for participants in HBS's executive education programmes. The building was a true joint venture. The $100-million project was funded up to a pre-determined $50 million by the Tata Group, while the remaining $50 million and any overruns were funded by HBS.

As with the $50 million in Tata Trusts' gift he had directed to Cornell in 2008, Ratan deemed the gift to HBS an appropriate return for what the institution had given him, Tata and India. Yet, at the 2013 Tata Hall dedication, Ratan frankly recalled 'his first weeks on the Harvard campus' in 1975 as 'confusing'. He confessed that he felt 'humiliated' by the impressive and overwhelming calibre of his fellow students. 'It was the only time in my life where I sat and crossed out day by day how many days were left before I could return to the normal world.'[18]

Coming from some other speaker, such stark confessions of self-doubt might seem a bit of a stretch. What Ratan felt in his three months at Harvard in 1975 was often genuinely stressful, and that he persevered despite his self-doubts is testimony to his strength of character. In later years, he realized the enormous benefits from the experience. In the end, his fortitude paid off, as he later explained: 'the confusion sort of disappeared', and he 'understood the magnitude' of what he 'had learned in a manner that I believe is not possible to do in places other than at this business school'.[19]

One business writer has described Ratan's experience at NELCO during a volatile period for Indian labour as a firing in a 'crucible', which 'produced a leader who was visionary, tough yet humane'. Ratan himself said, 'I learnt a lot. I don't think I could have learnt as much the hard way as I did in NELCO. I'm most grateful to the powers that be that they gave me NELCO and that they made me fight for three years, wondering where my next payroll was coming from, and [to fight] in a very competitive marketplace.'[20]

Ratan's Plan

In October 1981, a year after the NELCO lockout ended, forty-year-old Ratan was named chairman of Tata Industries by JRD.

Tata Industries had been set up in 1945 as a 'managing agency for the businesses it promoted'. The trouble was, as Ratan later explained, the chairmanship was largely 'a titular one' because, although 'Tata Industries had a great aura about it', it was, in fact, a 'company with no business activity' and no plan for any. Outside commentators in the press speculated that elevation to the chairmanship put Ratan in contention as a successor to Tata Sons chairman JRD, who was seventy-eight in 1981. Ratan himself did not take the likelihood of this ascension for granted.

What he believed was that the appointment placed a substantial burden on him to create a plan for Tata Industries and to define its place within the Tata Group. At what was therefore an acutely critical time, Ratan's mother, Soonoo, was diagnosed with cancer. In response, Ratan flew with her to New York, where she was treated at the famed Sloan-Kettering Institute. Remaining with her in the city for the next four months, Ratan used the time to lay out a plan not just for Tata Industries, but for the entire Tata Group.

He set down a vision intended to disrupt what had become a rather sleepy industrial giant. The company's somnolence had been encouraged by two things: firstly, there were India's onerous government regulations, which prevented Tata from expanding beyond India; and, secondly, there was the fact that Tata products were selling. True, the company was not growing, but it did manage to sell pretty much whatever it produced. This status quo was not sufficient for Ratan Tata. It was not that he wanted more for the sake of having more, but he believed the company had become complacent and was taking for granted its continued success, limited though it was.

'There was a need to look into the future and plan for it . . . to look at new business areas in a different kind of way,' he said. He believed that 'a lack of strategic planning has a profound effect on the position of a business organization in the marketplace and most of the problems of an organization can usually be traced to lack of planning'.[21]

Up to this point, the Tata companies had operated as traditional industrial companies. But the late 1970s, Ratan observed, saw an 'explosion of new emerging technologies in the West . . . the super mini and personal computers, driven by microprocessor advances, artificial intelligence, the convergence of computing and communication and information technology and biotechnology'.[22] There is truth in this, but most striking is that, to most observers, this truth would not be apparent for at least another decade.

The digital developments Ratan mentioned were indeed nascent as the 1970s gave way to the 1980s, but they would not begin to fully emerge until the late 1980s. Ratan was looking well ahead when he expressed his belief that 'the Tatas should be in these areas' of digital technology.

At the start of the 1980s, he argued that the Tata companies were 'among the few who would be willing and able to invest in these areas without expecting quick returns'. It was a statement typical of Ratan's leadership focus, which took a long-term view. He saw the Tatas' willingness to incur short-term expenses and even losses for the sake of achieving long-term innovation as one of the company's great strengths. This approach, he believed, was inherent in the founders' vision. In any case, his aspirations by the 1980s were not just for the sake of the company. They were national in scope. 'Why shouldn't Tatas enter those fields of recent technological advancement which have application potential *in India?*' he asked.[23] It really makes you realize how extraordinary a man JRD was. Here he was in his seventies promoting and pushing Tata in a whole new revolutionary direction.

Ratan's argument hit home with JRD, who believed it 'ideal for the Tatas to get the opportunities to enter high technology, high-risk industries'. Indeed, JRD saw this as 'almost a *duty* since only large groups can afford to take risks'. Nevertheless, all 'industries are eventually going to be high-tech . . . and India cannot afford to miss out on it'.[24]

Ratan interpreted JRD's response to his strategic plan as a mandate. By the early 1980s, he determined that the group should concentrate on 'telecommunications, oil exploration services, computers and its associated businesses', as well as 'advanced materials like special alloys and composites; and biotechnology and energy storage systems'. The Indian regulatory regime largely barred these areas from the private sector in the early 1980s, but Ratan, following JRD's lead, 'felt convinced that these were the areas Tatas must enter as they were the business of the future for India'. Not only did he see this risk-taking as a patriotic duty, but he also understood that the Indian government under the young, new prime minister, Rajiv Gandhi (1984–89), was becoming sufficiently liberalized, and obtaining the necessary licences would present no obstacle. In fact, Ratan later reported, the group was able to obtain '100 per cent of the licences for which it had applied'.[25]

Ratan made an impassioned and persuasive argument for his position. Despite this, his strategic plan failed to win acceptance among influential old-guard directors, who feared that the pursuit of new technologies would undercut their own interests. To them, Ratan's Strategic Plan for the future meant giving up the laissez-faire latitude they currently enjoyed. They had experienced significant success operating independently under the Tata umbrella, and they did not want to give up that independence by signing on to what they saw as the constraints of a central plan.

Ratan is an optimist, but he was and remains a pragmatist as well. Unable to win over the directors, he modified his plan to fit what he alone, as chairman of NELCO and of Tata Industries, could do. Using a limited capital investment, he established five new hi-tech enterprises under the aegis of Tata Industries: Tata Honeywell, Tata Telecom, Hitech Drilling, Tata Keltron and Tata Finance. Others were added later. He envisioned eventually dividing the Tata Group into eight distinct business areas: metals and associated industries; engineering; chemicals and agro-based industries; utilities; consumer products; services; high-tech industries; and international businesses. The last two would be directly under his charge.

Ratan in the Arena

In the meantime, in 1985, Ratan was appointed deputy chairman of TISCO (today known as Tata Steel). In September of the following year, he also became chairman of Air India, which had begun, under JRD, as Tata Airlines. But JRD was not moving Ratan into the chairmanship of Tata Sons just yet. Instead, in 1988, he decided to position Russi Mody, chairman of TISCO since 1984, as chairman of TELCO as well. Had this second chairmanship materialized, it would have given Mody the top spot in Tata's two largest companies, which, between them, represented half the group's total sales.

Mody was a Parsi, Indian-born but educated in England (St Cyprian's, Harrow, and Christ Church College, Oxford), who had worked his way up from the position of office assistant at TISCO. Following his elevation in TISCO, Mody boasted that he would shortly be also chosen to head TELCO, then considered to be the most forward-looking company in the group. The loose chatter alarmed some TELCO executives, including the company's serving chairman, Sumant Moolgaokar, who was widely credited with the building of TELCO from a sleepy railway locomotive manufacturer into a leading commercial vehicle producer. Plagued by ill health, Moolgaokar had been looking forward to the relief of retirement, but now reversed himself and refused to yield the chairmanship to Mody. Great pressure was brought on Ratan, who was being appointed deputy chairman, to refuse to serve under Moolgaokar. Out of enormous respect for him, however,

Ratan refused to undermine Moolgaokar's position, and Russi Mody finally had to withdraw from the battle. Eventually, Ratan became the deputy chairman of TELCO and finally its chairman, when Moolgaokar's failing health at last disenabled him to chair the company's board.

At this most difficult of junctures, labour relations at TELCO's massive truck plant in Pune began rapidly deteriorating. Even before Ratan was appointed deputy chairman, labour demonstrations had begun severely slowing production. In December 1988, when Moolgaokar's failing health prompted him to turn over the chairmanship to Ratan, the unrest was heating up. Outside observers, however, were not watching the labour situation as much as they were focusing on Ratan Tata. They were waiting to see how Mody, having so unexpectedly stumbled in his ascent to the post of JRD's heir apparent, would act to unseat him. But then the real assault came instead from a fiery internal union leader named Rajan Nair.

In March 1988, Nair was suspended after allegedly threatening to kill a plant security guard. Shortly after his suspension, he was fired. A few months later, Nair vowed that he would 'bring the TELCO management to its knees'.[26] To rally the workers behind him, he took up the cause of the still-unresolved wage agreement and presented himself as their representative in negotiations. Before talks could begin, however, Nair demanded that Tata officially recognize him as the leader of the plant's workers. Ratan, who had moved up from deputy chairman of TELCO to chairman in December 1988, refused to recognize Nair on two grounds: firstly, Nair was no longer employed by the company; and, secondly, he had a criminal record. Ratan made it clear that he and the rest of the management were very willing to negotiate with other union members, but could not accept Nair as the employees' representative.

Tensions mounted. On 31 January 1989, Ratan visited the Pune plant, where workers greeted him on the shop floor by laying down their tools. It was an ad hoc 'tools down' strike. In a stroke of bad timing, Pune police authorities decided to take Nair into 'preventive custody' on this very day. When news of this reached second-shift workers, they commandeered the buses that had been hired to transport them to the plant and drove them instead to central Pune, where they laid siege to the district courthouse until authorities set Nair free.

While this was going on, Ratan was meeting at the plant with one of Nair's aides and others. When Nair announced—falsely—that Ratan had ordered his arrest, the meeting broke down, and negotiations were suspended. On 15 March, 'Nair's men' targeted some twenty-two management personnel and 'rival unionists and assaulting and stabbing them in various parts of the city'. Nair did not deny this, but later claimed that 'the provocation was from the management because the previous day one of the TKS [TELCO Kamgar Sanghatana], the union he led, members was slapped on the shop floor'.[27]

The events that followed, Ratan says, were among the most painful and challenging he ever dealt with. Here he was, the newly appointed chairman of the company 'and suddenly your people are being stabbed. Your workers are being hit on the road and beaten up. The police are in the guy's pocket. You don't know what to do. You go to the shareholders meeting. The whole hall is full of these red handkerchief union leaders'—Nair and his loyalists wrapped red bandannas around their foreheads—'who are out to heckle your shareholders' meeting. And so, that was a time when I was nervous and new.'

But Ratan had not backed down from JRD and Mody. He did not now back down from Nair and TKS, even in the face of violent labour intimidation. 'If you put a gun to my head,' Ratan told Nair, 'you better be prepared to pull the trigger, as I will not be moving my head!' With that, he refused any further negotiation with Nair and his loyalists.

Ratan reached out instead to the rest of the workforce and to the local community. In a break with the company's conservative corporate tradition, he led management in a campaign to win over workers through face-to-face, one-on-one meetings. As for the community, which had a major stake in the prosperity of Tata's plants, Ratan used the media to shape favourable public opinion. As public relations campaigns go, it was a slow, methodical slog, but it paid off. On 19 September, TELCO management signed a three-year contract with TELCO Employees Union, a rival of TKS. Not only did the agreement offer a generous wage hike, but it also made a lump-sum payment of arrears. TELCO management reported that 1570 workers accepted the deal, to which Nair responded by leading his diehard supporters to Shaniwar Wada, where they intended to take refuge and stage a hunger strike.

The ruins of a Peshwa fortification built in Pune in 1732, Shaniwar Wada was a popular tourist site. Leading about 3000 workers, who identified their allegiance to their champion by tying around their foreheads bright red bandannas emblazoned with his name, Nair settled in for a long haul. When the strikers' fast passed the one-week mark, local government authorities feared that someone would die in Shaniwar Wada, touching off massive violence in Pune. Sharad Pawar, chief minister of the state of Maharashtra, brokered a meeting on 27 September 1989, between Nair and Ratan at the minister's official residence. Nair showed up late, and the meeting broke up soon after it got under way. Informed that the labour and management had failed to reach an agreement, Pawar launched Operation Crackdown. At 2.30 on the morning of 29 September, Maharashtra and Pune police rolled out to Shaniwar Wada aboard some eighty buses. After cordoning off the fort, they stormed it and removed the workers. Most were transported to various police stations in Pune, but Nair and his entourage were separately jailed on charges of attempted suicide and 'defying prohibitory orders'.[28]

The police action ended the strike, and by the close of 1989, daily production, which had fallen to a mere handful of vehicles during the worst of the labour action, recovered by November to an output of seventy vehicles a day (still well below the normal production of 140), with the number of employees on duty up from a skeleton-crew low of 700 to 2500.[29] The media was full of stories that told the story of Ratan's triumph over a rogue union leader. Ratan himself rejected this interpretation, however, and publicly commented that the recovery from the strike was a vindication of the principles and values Tata had held since the company's founding in the 19th century. He gave full credit to courageous workers who faced down intimidation and to white-collar office staff, who 'were manning machines and people in the accounts department [who] were moving materials'. We started producing vehicles with about 800 people. I think that the kind of spirit that was created in Pune then [during the strike] would never have been created were it not for the conflict.' Ratan conceded to the press that it was a victory for the company and its team, but it was a victory 'caused by circumstances which were, ironically, created by Rajan Nair'. He spoke about the 'sense of friendliness' that now prevailed in the plant. 'I can walk around the shop floor and talk to people. They come and talk to me. We smile and shake hands.'[30]

Ratan is often described as a modest, reserved and even shy man. Colleagues describe him as eminently approachable and very affable. For him, conversation, smiling and shaking hands with workers came naturally. He discovered that he was very good at the one-on-one management approach, the approach that treats employees as members and teammates. It is also clear that he took away from the difficult, at times violent, strike a valuable lesson. 'Perhaps,' he told the press, 'we took our workers for granted. We assumed that we were doing all that we could for them when probably we were not.' As for Nair, Ratan recognized him for what he was—the product of dysfunctional management. 'We gave Rajan Nair—or any name—a chance to come and do what he did.'[31]

Chairman Ratan

Understandably enough, Ratan's successful resolution of the long labour crisis at TELCO did not sit well with the man who had counted on having this job. Russi Mody had been on the verge of claiming the two major chairmanships that would have put him unassailably in position to take over as chairman of Tata Sons when JRD stepped down. His having fumbled and thereby lost the TELCO chairmanship to Ratan was bad enough, but Ratan's performance in resolving the labour crisis made it even worse. Mody had enjoyed a reputation as the Tata Group's go-to leader in the field of labour relations. Now it was the quiet, unassuming Ratan Tata who emerged as a strong manager in a crisis.

And it had to do with more than overcoming one particular crisis. While the media continued to portray him—with admiration—as a tough manager of labour, Ratan himself, quietly, out of the limelight, pursued a strategy of rebuilding and improving labour relations at TELCO for the long term. Crisis management became a platform from which he could do more than merely prepare to fight the next fire. Ratan wanted instead to prevent future fires by building a culture of trust between management and labour. The strategy worked. On 31 March 1991, the end of the year's first quarter, TELCO, so recently crippled by strikes, beat out TISCO—chaired by Russi Mody—for first place among India's private sector companies. As measured by sales, it was TELCO, not TISCO, that was now the biggest single company in India. TELCO sales rose by nearly a third, before-tax profits rose 58 per cent and vehicle production hit 81,931 units, a 26 per cent rise.[32]

Some crises make a man. Some break him. The long, violent labour dispute at TELCO threatened to break Ratan, but ended up making him—making him the successor to J.R.D. Tata as chairman of Tata Sons on 25 March 1991. On 10 November 1993, eighty-nine-year-old JRD—who in just nineteen days would succumb to a kidney infection in a hospital in Geneva, Switzerland—spoke of why he had, two years earlier, chosen to pass the torch to Ratan. 'I knew what Ratan's strengths and abilities were, and I was totally convinced that he was the best man to succeed me, not only because of his abilities, but [also] because he totally shared my sense of values.' Commenting on this, Ratan Tata agreed that 'it is only right' to put so much emphasis on values, 'considering that values are fundamental to the Tata ethos'. But the fact was that Ratan had come into the Tata companies way back in 1962 already in possession of those values. Three decades later, when he became chairman of Tata Sons at the age of fifty-three, he had learnt something else: that 'values by themselves should be subservient to corporate performance'.[33] An expression of the delicate balance between philanthropic ethos and competitive capitalism, the balance at the core of the Tata companies, this was a position Jamsetji Tata himself would have embraced passionately.

4

Mission and Values

*I would love to see the disparity between the rich and poor [in India]
reduced. If you have a billion people that should be our strength.*
—Ratan Tata, interview with Damien Whitworth, 2006[1]

India first glimmered as the future 'Jewel in the Crown' of
the British Empire in 1835, when colonial administrators
discovered that the hillsides of Assam, the frontier region of
north-east India, were covered with a wild-growing evergreen
shrub that botanists call *Camellia sinensis* and everyone else refers
to as the tea tree, tea shrub or just plain tea plant. In 1849, after
a New Jersey-born carpenter found metallic yellow flakes in the
American River near Coloma, California, there was a Gold Rush.
In 1835, in India, it was a Tea Rush. The promise of fortunes to
be made from the Assam hillsides catalysed the creation, in 1858,
of the British Raj, the rule over the Indian subcontinent by the
British Crown.

A full 142 years later, in 2000, under the chairmanship of Ratan
Tata, the Raj, which had ended in 1947 with Indian Independence,
was suddenly rewound and run backwards. That year, the Tata
Group acquired Tetley, the biggest teabag brand of the former

British Empire. It was the largest foreign acquisition ever by an Indian company, and, six years later, when journalist Damian Whitworth called at the Taj Mahal Palace—the iconic Tata hotel in Mumbai—to interview the Tata chairman for *The Times*, he beheld Ratan 'in an opulent suite', gazing 'out across the Arabian Sea towards the West', sipping 'ice tea (Tetley's, of course) and reflecting on the deal'.[2]

Whitworth asked him if he enjoyed 'the irony of an Indian company buying Britain's leading tea brand? 'Yes,' he replied then quickly changed the subject. 'Tata is too shrewd and too shy to be caught gloating about his successes like some territory-grabbing East India Company nabob.'[3]

Maybe there really was a touch of shrewdness about Ratan's reserve on that occasion—but, if so, it was only a touch. Damian Whitworth himself wrote that before he met Ratan, he was attending a party thrown by the head of Air India, the state-owned national airline that had been founded in 1932 by J.R.D. Tata as Tata Airlines, India's first commercial air carrier. 'Le tout Mumbai was there,' Whitworth wrote, 'and as the wine flowed, there was only one mysterious absentee, Ratan Tata himself.' When he asked about this, the revellers laughed: 'He's a recluse. He doesn't exactly do the cocktail circuit.'"

They talked fondly of Ratan, but clearly regarded him as an eccentric. 'He sometimes drives himself!' reported one member of this chauffeur-driven set. Randhir Kapoor, the Bollywood film-star-turned-producer, recalled going to the barber in the hotel at the same time as Tata. 'He paid for his own haircut,' he said, amazed but approving.'[4]

With most of Tata Sons owned by charitable trusts, Ratan and the other Tatas are wealthy but far from being multibillionaires. Ratan was raised in what amounted to a palace by the grand lady of one of the wealthiest families in India. 'And yet,' Whitworth writes, 'if you look at his lifestyle now, he lives like any professional manager—actually, all the top corporate honchos I know, have lifestyles vastly in excess of Ratan's. He's lived for the last few years in a comfortable flat with a small garden for Tito and Tango [his dogs], on the coast a few miles from the Taj Mahal Palace hotel. The apartment is owned by the Tata Group and upon his death will be returned to the group. I conducted most of our interviews at the apartment. It is the home of a bachelor who loves reading and dogs, certainly not the home of the head of India's largest conglomerate.' Ratan admitted, 'Yes, I did grow up amidst a lot of wealth. But don't forget that I spent ten years in America trying to live on the Reserve Bank's allowances . . . and . . . and the money was never enough. So I had to take all kinds of jobs, including washing dishes, to make ends meet. That sort of thing helps you forget that your family is rich quite quickly.'[5]

If this modesty—an ethos of drive-yourself-and-pay-for-your-own-haircut—seemed remarkable in the chairman of the greatest company in India, it was, Whitworth implied, entirely of a piece with the radically unconventional company itself. Whitworth quoted a 'well-known Indian investigative journalist', who had pointed out to him that the Tata Group was different from other companies in the country. 'They refuse to take bribes. That's very unusual.' Ratan himself laid down as a principle: 'Corruption is rife . . . We will not submit ourselves to corruption.'[6]

And that is not all. Whitworth judged the 'Tata group . . . possibly unique among global corporations in its approach to its workers. Take Ratan Tata's restructuring of the steel division. With investment in mechanization and adoption of new processes, Tata Steel would now require far fewer people to run the plant than it had before. There were great uncertainty and unrest about a possible massive layoff of employees. But instead of simply laying off thousands of employees, Ratan was able to get the Union's agreement on a voluntary retirement scheme, wherein the employees retired per the company's plans, vacating company accommodation and related facilities and leaving Jamshedpur. In return for this, Ratan had offered to continue payment of their basic salary until their age of retirement. This averted a major dispute involving a demand for employment to the next generation of employees. The payment of the basic wage until retirement was unbelievably lower in cost than holding surplus manpower to appease the Unions or long drawn out agitation and discord between the workers and the management.'[7] In doing this, Ratan demonstrated that his values proceed unbroken from those of Jamsetji Tata and his sons, who laid the foundation for an exuberantly capitalist enterprise that nevertheless defined corporate social responsibility not as a fringe-benefit by-product of business success, but as the indispensable driver of that success, the reason for a company to do business.

'The statistics are chilling,' Ratan said in 2006. 'We [in India] produce 18 million new people every year. That's [almost] one Australia each year. I would love to see the disparity between the rich and poor reduced. If you have a billion people that should be our strength.'[8]

Mission

Chapter 3 brought the career of Ratan Tata to 1991, the year he became chairman of Tata Sons while also serving as chair of the Tata Trusts, the first and only person to simultaneously control both major trusts and be chairman of Tata Sons. Before we follow his career at the helm of the company, let's take this chapter to pause for an overview of the mission and values he brought to his chairmanship.

When he spoke to Damien Whitworth in 2006, he spoke of reducing the gap between the rich and the poor in India, not just in the name of social justice but to make the challenging fact of a billion-person population the nation's greatest strength rather than its greatest vulnerability. Like the founders of the company, Ratan is an Indian patriot and nationalist. He admits, albeit ever-so-quietly, to a certain satisfaction in claiming British Tetley as an Indian company. Yet, also like Jamsetji, Ratanji and Dorabji, he is not *simply* a nationalist. The year before his *Times Magazine* interview, he shared his global vision for Tata in a blog titled 'A World to Win'.[9]

> [I]t is not globalization, as is commonly understood, which we seek to achieve. Globalization is typically equated with having a presence in every continent. That is not our intention: we seek to grow in select geographies. To that extent what we are attempting is simply a greater internationalization of our businesses. Where this thrust is different from the past is that it goes beyond exports: we will want to be part of the communities in which we operate.

Those last dozen words are critical to understanding the mission and values Ratan believes are at the heart of the Tata companies:

> Each company should increase its international footprint as part of its own growth strategy. Companies will need to be very selective about the geographies they are entering. They should go abroad only when they believe they can establish a meaningful presence in that territory . . .
>
> We would like our companies to establish themselves in different geographies as local companies contributing to the local community and participating in the development of those countries. We should be a part of those nations, make a contribution with our products and services—either from India or locally produced— and be viewed as part of those countries, enjoying the same degree of trust we do in India.

We do not want to be seen to be transplanting India into those countries. The right model is to adapt ourselves to the culture of the local place. If we are going to China, we should have a Chinese face, and not an Indian face in China. We should be perceived as a Chinese company, but owned in India. That, in my view, is the path we need to take . . .

'We believe that our presence will be much more substantial in developing countries in Asia, Africa and parts of Eastern Europe,' Ratan concluded, saying, 'Investments may be more of an exception in the developed countries, except in areas like IT services.'

Ratan does not explicitly condemn the British for having failed to build their empire with the goal of making life better for the Crown's colonial subjects. He does make clear, however, that the Tata 'empire' does have that purpose. A leading goal of the Tata companies' globalization is making life better for those mostly developing countries into which Tata has expanded.

Values

In its broadest outlines, the Tata mission has not varied since the days of the founders. Simply put, the ethos of the company yokes capitalism to philanthropy, doing well by doing good, doing business in ways that make the lives of others better. Originally, the focus was exclusively on India. As the company has grown and as Indian commercial laws were liberalized to permit the globalization of Indian companies, the focus has broadened to more general philanthropy. Towards the end of his chairmanship, Ratan spoke of doing business in developing parts of the world. This would not only profitably serve underserved markets but also create employment and other opportunities in poor nations. However the mission has evolved, it has always been inseparable from a set of values, which are simultaneously personal and corporate. They are values that cannot be articulated abstractly, but must be worked and lived.

The Tata values can be distilled to a handful: discipline, respect for the test of time, honour tradition but say no to the status quo, honour the customer, promote belonging, value quality in people, exercise honest optimism.

Discipline

Spend any considerable time with Ratan, and you draw two apparently contradictory conclusions about him. First, there is a stately calm about the man. Second, there is a fierce discipline. Ratan was once asked the source of his discipline, which was likely fostered by the formative role of his formidable grandmother, Lady Navajbai. In describing her, he said, 'She was very strict, and she expected to have a disciplined household. She was also very kind and very large-hearted, but she did expect to have a certain decorum, discipline, above all dignity. She would not permit any indignity to happen. She really raked us over the coals if any of us did something that was dishonourable—even as kids.'

She instilled discipline 'on a continuous basis', Ratan explained.

Lady Navajbai let nothing slip by. The discipline she nurtured, however, was not based not on punishment but accountability—on setting goals and keeping score. For Ratan, this has carried over into adult life in his habit of giving himself daily to-do lists.

'I constantly prepare to-do lists,' he said, as he produced a small handwritten list of about fifteen things he planned to get done on that particular day.

He explained that he typically created his to-do list early in the morning, 'usually at two in the morning or four in the morning', he said. 'Sometimes, I wake up and I remember I didn't do X and Y, so I pull out a piece of paper and write it down.' Napoleon spoke of possessing 'two o'clock in the morning courage'. So, we discover that Ratan Tata believes in the importance 'of 'two o'clock in the morning discipline'.[10]

Respect for the Test of Time

Ratan does not talk about 'tradition' when the subject turns to the legacy of Jamsetji, his sons and their successors. What he says instead is that 'the Tata organization has withstood the test of time in terms of its direction'. 'Test of time' is not synonymous with 'tradition'. It has even less in common with reverence for the status quo. What the test of time concerns is always taking the long view.[11]

'We're a group that stays with it,' Ratan explains. 'We fight our difficult periods, and we have surprised people with our success.' He cites Tata Steel, which was at one point in great peril. In response, Sir Dorabji, took out a loan, quite literally 'pledging his family's jewels on it . . . to keep the Tata Group going.'

In more recent times, during Ratan's watch as group chairman, Jaguar Land Rover fell into crisis. 'After we bought JLR, the banking sector collapsed and the economy of the UK and the European Union collapsed also. The easiest thing for us to do would have been to close down new projects because R&D would have been the first place to cut costs. Instead, we pumped into JLR more than we paid for the company. We bought the company for $1.6 billion, and we pumped in over $2 billion after that, most of it invested in research and development. The result was that, when we came out of the recession, we were not a company that had two ten-year-old products to offer, but four or five products hot in the pipeline.'

Ratan's approach was, wherever possible, to trust the test of time and position the company for the future. One of his chief criticisms of Cyrus Mistry was what Ratan called his mindset of

'I can't run this. Sell it. Close it down.' This, Ratan explained, isn't 'what Tata has been all about'. He admits, 'If a company doesn't make it, we have closed companies down. We have sold companies. But we make a damn good effort to turn them back into profit. See, we've always been somewhat closer to national assets, building and operating national assets, power, and steel. If we could have been in railways, we would have been in railways, too.'

When it was pointed out that Tata was in airlines until Air India was nationalized, Ratan comments, 'Yeah, we were in local transport. And we were making rails also, but we weren't in railways. But our objective has always been *not* to put people out of work, *not* to close things down unless it became absolutely necessary.'

Honour Tradition but Say No to the Status Quo

Taking the long view and positioning for the future are aspects of the Tata tradition that both JRD and Ratan emphasized. Yet both chairmen also valued innovation. The roots of this may be seen in Jamsetji Tata. In the context of Victorian India, he was an essential innovator, who pulled India into the Industrial Revolution, yet his values were rooted in his Zoroastrian faith, which fostered an ethic of helping others. Ratan does not see these values as ancient, or modern, or even religious. They are timeless, and they are right. JRD, Ratan points out, set these down years ago in a document he called 'Guiding Principles'. To this day, Ratan keeps a copy close to him:

1. Nothing worthwhile is ever achieved without deep thought and hard work;
2. One must think for oneself and never accept at their face value slogans and catchphrases to which, unfortunately, our people are too easily susceptible;

3. One must forever strive for excellence, or even perfection, in
    any task however small, and never be satisfied with the second
    best;

4. No success or achievement in material terms is worthwhile
    unless it serves the needs or interests of the country and its
    people and is achieved by fair and honest means;

5. Good human relations not only bring great personal rewards
    but also are essential to the success of any enterprise.[12]

Yet, while Ratan honours tradition, he has no use at all for the status
quo. He feels fortunate to have ascended to the Tata chairmanship
in 1991, the beginning of the administration of Prime Minister
P.V. Narasimha Rao and finance minister Dr Manmohan Singh,
who initiated the 'economic liberalization' of India. 'Many of my
comrades in industry were spending their time with the government
trying to ensure the protection of the status quo,' Ratan says. 'I,
on the other hand, was running around encouraging more to be
opened up.'

The Nano

Ratan always championed innovation—not just for the sake of
innovation, but as a blow against the deadening complacency of
status quo leadership. He has a personal passion for innovation, and
if you can combine innovation with social causes and cars—about
which he is equally passionate—you will usually get his attention.

Many visitors to India are struck by the incessant honking of
horns. Vehicles, including motorbikes, are everywhere, with entire
families on board. Husband driving, two children and the mother
in the rear. If there is a helmet in this picture, it is invariably on
the husband's head.

Ratan saw these scenes daily, and became obsessed with the
idea of producing a safe, affordable car that would get families

off motorbikes. He once commented, 'My happiest time at work was when we designed and launched the INDICA—India's first Indian designed, engineered and manufactured car. Another exciting period was when we developed the NANO, which was a four-door family car which would sell for $1500 and would give the opportunity to many families to own their own car. While the Indica had a high market share and had a market life of several years, the Nano, unfortunately, for various reasons, did not enjoy a meaningfully large market share or market life.'[13]

Although Ratan might consider the launch of the Indica the happiest time, outsiders might scratch their head at that statement, since the Nano turned out to be a source of much angst for Ratan. Cyrus Mistry even used it as an example of a corporate fiasco and another reason why he, Cyrus Mistry, should never have been terminated.

But, if you look carefully, the entire Nano episode is in many ways a microcosm of Ratan's life. Examine it in detail, and you discover the many facets of Ratan's personality. The Nano project demonstrated his determination and focus, yet it also showed that he can be very stubborn, some would argue to a fault. It also showed that he can be overly optimistic, even after almost fifty years in business. The challenges that clustered around the choice of location for building the car in Singur—which touched off an eminent domain scandal when the West Bengal state government moved to forcibly purchase 997 acres of farmland for the plant[14]— also demonstrated his lack of political finesse, something his father, Naval, a consummate politician, possessed in abundance.

For those, particularly in the West, who are not familiar with it, the Tata Nano went into production in 2008—and continues currently as the Tata GenX Nano—as an affordable alternative to motor scooters and small motorcycles. While it is very small— 87.8-inch wheelbase and 122 inches in total length, powered by a two-cylinder aluminium engine—it has four doors and a full backseat, making it a 'family car' and therefore a genuine four-wheel alternative to the dangerously overloaded motor scooter.

In an earlier interview in 2005 with Vir Sanghvi in the *Hindustan Times*, Ratan explained how the Indica came to be developed: 'I always thought we should build a small car. But foreign small or medium-sized cars are all meant to be self-driven, which means that nobody pays any attention to the back seat, which sort of sinks down when you sit in it. I wanted a car that could be chauffeur-driven, where the back wasn't too low. I wanted to build a modern version of the Ambassador at a competitive price. He was referring to the Hindustan Ambassador, which had begun manufacture in 1958 and was still very much in production in 2005 (its run ended in 2014). A four-door compact sedan, the Ambassador was much beloved as the 'king of Indian roads'. Creating something competitive with it at a radically affordable price was Ratan's aspiration. Making it happen turned out to be a very tall order.[15]

'Even within Tatas,' Ratan told Vir Sanghvi, 'people kept asking me to distance myself from the project so that when it failed, I wouldn't be stuck with the blame. And when I refused to do that, they distanced themselves from me.' Sanghvi noted that his subject smiled before continuing: 'But it was a good thing in retrospect because I got very involved with the team and we worked very closely together and were much more motivated as a result.'[16]

A year later, Tata Sons group publications chief, Christabelle Noronha, interviewed Ratan.[17] 'One of your passions,' she observed, 'is to address the customer at the bottom of the pyramid, by bringing out high-quality products at local prices. This has led to Tata companies taking up projects like the small car and no-frills hotels.'

Ratan responded: 'I think industries in India, by and large, have mostly been looking at the small section of the population at the top of the pyramid, the 200–250 million middle class that is the consuming public. That's an acceptable model because of its consonance with the scale and size of our companies.'

Ratan continued: 'The 400 million and more just below them is what we have to target, because they are potential consumers. Can we go and cater to that marketplace? I think there is an opportunity there. But it should not be, cannot be, that low-cost products come to mean inferior or sub-standard products and services; definitely not. The aim is to create products for that larger segment—good and robust products that we are able to produce innovatively and get to the marketplace at lower costs.'

Ratan noted that Indian companies were falling all over themselves to woo the urban customer, but the rural marketplace was addressed in a very insignificant way. 'Yes, soap may go there, and cloth will go and maybe beverages like tea and coffee will go, but are we really catering to that segment of the market? I don't think we are. We're only taking the frills out of products and offering a lower price, not really looking at the needs of rural consumers and developing products especially for them.' With the Nano, Ratan aimed to reach the 'man on a two-wheeler with a child standing in front, his wife sitting behind'. He continued: 'Add to that the wet roads—a family in potential danger.' His aim was 'to make a contribution to making life safer for them'.

He also saw manufacturing the Nano as a chance to reach the bottom of the pyramid. His original intention was to build the Nano plant 'in West Bengal because I think the eastern part of the country has been ignored industrially and, contrary to the belief of most people, the industrial climate in West Bengal is really good and the leadership is inspiring'. In response to Ratan's initiative to build a plant in West Bengal, the state offered a choice from among six sites.

So what, exactly, went wrong with the choice of Singur?

In reality, it could have and should have been an excellent choice. The problem was that the West Bengal government, since Independence, had been ruled by a very Communist-leaning administration. As a result, there were few entrepreneurial initiatives and the state was lagging behind in terms of economic growth. The difficulty was that the government offered to lease the land to Tata Motors, but they revived an 1894 eminent domain law to acquire land from the local farmers through compulsory sale.

Ratan and the board of Tata Motors believed that the government of West Bengal could deliver on their commitments; after all, the economic benefits to this chronically poor state would have been huge. In short order, however, Tata and the state were overwhelmed by opposition from the farmers slated for displacement by plant construction. Led by Mamata Banerjee, a very capable, eloquent politician and activist, the West Bengal farmers launched a Save Our Farmland movement, which gained the support of a number of prominent Indian social activists. When the Tatas prevailed against objections and obtained permission to begin construction, Banerjee called for a state-wide *bandh*, or general strike, which included her own twenty-five-day hunger strike. The area fenced off for the construction of the plant had to be continuously guarded, and violent clashes occurred with alarming regularity. Despite this, construction was under way by January 2007.[18] The violence caused Ratan much personal distress. It brought back memories of his conflict with Rajan Nair.[19] That conflict produced one of the most famous quotes associated with Ratan Tata: 'If you put a gun to my head, you better be prepared to pull the trigger, as I will not be moving my head!'[20]

When asked if there had been another time, other than the confrontation with Rajan Nair during the violence and strikes at TELCO when Ratan used the gun-to-my-head line, he replied, 'Yes. I told Mamata Banerjee the same thing!'[21]

'I guess she pulled the trigger,' said Ratan. After having built the plant, decided to close it.[22] He was very emotional about the decision to close the plant in Singur, as he felt that West Bengal badly needed the economic stimulus that the plant would bring. In the end, however, he was politically outmanoeuvred by Mamata Banerjee, who used the victory to win a landslide at the next election and ended up becoming First Minister of West Bengal.

Ironically, sometime later and once in office, she realized the huge loss to the state, and she offered Tata Motors 1000 acres in West Midnapore. By then it was far too late; Ratan and the board had moved the plant to Gujarat. Banerjee won the battle but lost the war.

Moving the plant to Gujarat enabled them to buy the land needed. As a technological innovator on a social scale, Ratan takes a holistic view when possible. If the Nano had been offered as an alternative to dangerously inadequate personal transportation for a large segment of customers that Indian businesses had underserved or altogether ignored, Ratan also looked to the exploration of energy alternatives to address the nation's acute energy problems. He said that there is no time to be complacent: 'I don't think we have been doing enough in the field of alternative energy. It's still a secondary business; we need to put it into prime focus.' His suggested focus was an area ripe for innovation— hydrogen. 'Addressing stationary power and finding ways to generate hydrogen and use it as feedstock to power stations might be a good way to help solve the energy problem.'[23] Today, Ratan believes that we need to explore all energy alternatives and is very supportive of the joint venture with MDI from France and believes that some form of hybrid air car will be available within three years.[24]

With the Nano, Ratan pushed the envelope, much as did in various other parts of his life. He trusted people, and there were many mistakes made. Apart from the political mistakes, he had made simple marketing blunders.[25] He said that it 'was a huge mistake to brand the Nano as "The World's Cheapest Car". People don't want to be seen driving the world's cheapest car!' Nevertheless, despite much criticism and many obstacles, Ratan persevered and came up with a different solution.

Instead of abandoning the project, as Cyrus Mistry wanted, Tata Motors has entered into a joint venture with Jayem Automotives, an Indian auto parts manufacturer, in which Tata Motors will supply the Nano shell and assemble a new electric version of a revamped Nano called the Neo. The first 450 Neos have already been produced and have been designated as taxis.[26]

Honour the Customer

Ratan continually questions the status quo in the interest of customers, whether it is the underserved customers at the 'base of the pyramid' or consumers in general. When asked about his vision for Tata's future, he responded without hesitation: 'First of all, Tata companies must be seen as fair players to their customers. That is exceedingly important. I couldn't tell you precisely what businesses I would like to be in or see ourselves being in, but whatever businesses we are in, we want to be perceived to be a company that is fair to the consumer, fair to the supplier and fair to all stakeholders. We want consumers to presume that when they hear or see the name Tata attached to a business—let's say a new business—they think, well, at least they will be honest. They will be fair and just to us. We'll support them.'[27]

Honouring the customer—making the customer king, as Ratan sometimes puts it—does not come naturally to Indian companies. 'For many years, India was and has been in [an economically] protected environment. Tata Group companies, in many cases, were in a seller's market, and we were very successful in that seller's market. I think that, broadly, we were perceived as being fair and just to our customers, with our products being backed by a concern for quality. We have been credited with being ahead of the times.'[28] Today, however, this basic degree of regard for the customer is regarded by markets as mere table stakes. It is no longer sufficient as a value proposition.

As the effects of India's 'economic liberalization' set it, Indian companies began to liberalize as well. 'This has resulted in competition between Indian companies, as also from joint ventures established in the country by foreign companies. And now, with the World Trade Organisation and the market opening up from outside, we . . . face competition from global players.' Ratan acknowledges the need for 'a new approach to recognising what the marketplace wants, and how to establish not just customer relations but customer loyalty.'[29]

Ratan became concerned that the Tata companies operating 'as individual brands, or variants of a Tata brand' needed to identify more closely with the central Tata brand, so that customer loyalty can be built both bigger and stronger. He cautions, however, that 'brand by itself does not automatically usher in customer loyalty or strengthen customer relations. That is a human interface, and it embodies courtesy and fairness; it also embodies timely actions in terms of meeting customer needs. It strives at all times for customer loyalty, rather than mere customer satisfaction.' Yet, while today's customers increasingly demand and expect to be treated like kings, Ratan is always wary about certain Tata policies that 'are framed almost on the basis . . . that a customer has to prove his bona 'fides'.

'That is what we need to change. Where we have direct dealings with our customers, it is important that, at the middle-management levels, they are shown courtesy, dealt with fairly and made to feel that they are receiving the attention they deserve. The interface with the customer should be a seamless one.' He concludes bluntly, '[It is] part of the Indian psyche to say, "I will treat important people with great courtesy, and I will treat everyone else, not with scorn, but as second-class citizens. I will show my superiority as an individual." I think this is really terrible . . .'[30]

The antidote to this commercially and socially corrosive attitude is to treat all customers equally—that is, with the greatest respect. Beyond this, it is also essential to practise innovative and imaginative empathy with customers. The better you can understand their needs, the better your company will perform. 'Theoretically, the top managers of a company should take up the role of that ideal customer: they should be driving their competitors' vehicles, they should be driving the best-of-breed vehicles, and they should be making cost comparisons. They must have an idea of what they, as customers, expect from a Tata vehicle. And they should try to ensure that the product is within the price parameters a customer would pay for.'

At the same time, top managers need to face reality objectively. 'While a top manager should be the ideal customer, he should also be the greatest critic of his company's products. If the CEO compromises, or is only looking at the margins, then even if he is successful, the company's success will be short-lived. That is because the market will determine whose product works and whose product is successful. That in turn will bring everything else into play.'[31]

Promote Belonging

A company's brand is its identity. It encapsulates the firm's value proposition. In a 2003 interview, Tata's Christabelle Noronha asked Ratan how Tata employees can be made sensitive to the value of the brand.[32] 'Firstly,' Ratan replied, 'I don't think you can sensitize employees, in the sense that your product has to be successful, and you have to have pride in that product. You may say that a product cannot be successful unless you create a sense of pride in your employees. I think that there is an issue

Ratan at the launch of the Indica in December 1998, at the time India's most modern car.

Ratan in the cockpit as he prepares to fly.

Ratan posing for pictures during an interview with a business magazine, 1983.

Ratan in a casual pose, 1983–84.

Ratan in 1988. Photo by Elaine Jones.

Ratan and Jimmy in happier times.

Ratan in a pensive mood with Tito, 1974.

Ratan in a playful mood with Tito, 1974.

Ratan shaking hands.

Jamsetji Tata, bearded patriarch, with his family (circa 1900).

Young Ratan with his family.

Ratan with sisters Shireen and Deanna, Boston, 1976.

Ratan with his sisters Shireen and Deanna.

Ratan and Jimmy at the Tata House, 1947.

Ratan with his father, Naval, and brother Jimmy, pictured while leaving for university in the US, 1954.

of involvement: employees at all levels should feel motivated and committed to making a product successful. The shop floor needs to be motivated too. They need to feel that they are part of what the companies do.' To create this feeling, 'managers should talk about the new products that they are in the process of launching and give all employees a sense of involvement'. Ratan suggests creating special employee badges promoting the new product, or 'labels on their sleeves [or] special caps'. The object is to create 'a cadre of people who [are] all excited about the [new] project' or product. Much as word-of-mouth remains the most powerful marketing tool among consumers, converting a 'cadre' of key employees into champions for a product or project is a supremely effective means of creating enthusiasm for a new initiative, project or product.

Building a sense of excitement, loyalty and belonging must go beyond mere morale-raising symbols. 'We need to make it our responsibility to expose employees to the company holistically. They need to recognise the need to earn the return for the person who has invested in their company. This kind of awareness can perhaps be built best by moving people into positions where they have to face different constituents.' Ratan is not shy about pointing out to some of his colleagues, 'You don't have to face the shareholders when you make a loss. I do. Maybe you should stand up one day and face the shareholders for what you've deprived them of.'

In big organizations especially, there is an ever-present danger of individuals and even whole departments becoming counterproductively siloed. This, naturally, makes achieving a holistic vision virtually impossible. 'Selectively involving people in shareholder meets, investor conferences and dealer meets will help in exposing them to different situations that they may face,' Ratan believes. He has sent 'plant people to customer-service operations to enable them to see the different kinds of problems people face in the field'. If they are not afforded this perspective, it becomes a situation of 'their production and somebody else's problem'. The only effective argument against this shirking of responsibility is to persuade employees 'to believe that they are responsible for the company'. To create such a conviction often requires a change in perspective that only a trip outside the silo can bring about; however, Ratan believes that the culture of belonging, of shared responsibility, must begin with the CEO, who 'has to be concerned with all kinds of things, not just the bottom line, production figures or the company's image. A holistic concern should be created.'

Creating a sense of belonging, a willingness to share responsibility for the destiny of the company and its brand, requires even more than a holistic vision of the organization. It requires both management and labour to reject absolutely all manner of political, social and cultural discrimination. When the Indian government was considering imposing caste-based employment quotas on companies, Ratan responded resolutely: 'I feel very sensitive and concerned about people who have been traditionally deprived, but the word "caste" is not in my vocabulary at all. So, as far as I'm concerned, our employees are our employees. We have never tried to determine what caste they come from or even what religion they come from, although sometimes a name may betray what somebody's religious roots are.'[33]

As a member of the Parsi community, Ratan was raised with a strong bias in favour of helping the poor. 'I believe that we, that is, Indian industry, should have the responsibility of doing something for the traditionally deprived, but quotas are not an answer. What is needed is to give people an equal opportunity, which they do not have today. And I think that equal opportunity will not come from quotas; it will come from having more primary schools for them, perhaps finding solutions that will enable their families to send them to school, instead of leaving them in a situation in which they have to pull them out of school to send them to work.

I believe that equal opportunity will come from creating vocational training for them so that they can master a trade.'[34]

In the recent past, Ratan has proposed government legislation 'to help create enterprises . . . run by the underprivileged.' For instance, he suggests requiring 'industry to buy 5–10 per cent of their raw materials and components from companies run by underprivileged entrepreneurs, subject to quality and price being equal. That would be a healthy thing because we would then be creating enterprises, creating genuine prosperity. You buy from them and they become useful citizens and they grow.'

Indeed, under Ratan's leadership, Tata Tea sold 'our entire plantation in south India to our workers. What we have now is a company owned and managed by workers, and we buy tea from that company.' Ratan admits that there were sceptics 'who felt that we were making losses in the plantations and we passed on our losses to our workers. What has actually happened is that once the workers became owners, the plantations made a profit.' It is a 'true win-win situation on both sides. In time, we will have some very prosperous individuals who will own a piece of a tea estate or a set of tea estates. They will make their own destiny . . . And if they become really wealthy, I think all of us at Tata Tea will be extremely happy.' In this, Ratan speaks from personal feeling: 'I get enormous pleasure from seeing the uplift of an underprivileged or poor person. I feel elated when I walk on the street and see someone who pushes a handcart talking on a cell phone. Prosperity is spreading.'[35]

Value Quality in People

When asked about the people who have shaped his thinking, Ratan generally mentions J.R.D. Tata first. Others include the capitalist philanthropist Chuck Feeney (Chapter 3); John F. Kennedy ('I never met him but his thinking influenced me in many ways');

Henry Schacht, chairman of Cummins and Lucent Technologies; MIT professor and founder of the Bose Corporation, Amar Bose; and Jean Riboud, the French socialist, World War II–era anti-Nazi resistance leader, and chairman of Schlumberger, the largest oilfield services company in the world. 'There's a common thread these people share—strong values. They have the integrity of a high order and a very forceful social consciousness in terms of what their corporations do. In addition, they are warm, thoughtful and caring human beings.'

Besides individuals with these qualities, Ratan admires 'people who are very successful'. To this, he adds an important caveat: 'But if that success has been achieved through too much ruthlessness, then I may admire that person, but I can't respect him.'[36]

Of all the personal qualities Ratan values most, the one business demands most, is what he describes as a 'self-imposed . . . framework of ethics, values, fairness and objectivity'. Ratan warns that 'you cannot impose [such a framework] on yourself forcibly because it has to become an integral part of you'. It is something that 'has to go through your mind at the time of every decision, or most decisions'. It requires you to ask: 'Does this stand the test of public scrutiny in terms of what I said earlier? As you think the decision through, you have to automatically feel that this is wrong, incorrect, or unfair. You have to think of the advantages or disadvantages to the segments involved, be it employees or stakeholders.'[37]

Add to all of these qualities, one more. Call it a drive to create complete perfection.

'I often get frustrated by acts or implementations that are incomplete or imperfect, where I feel someone has not thought something through and has just done the job mechanically . . . I appreciate a person who does a little bit of overkill, even though it is not necessary. I get very, very frustrated and upset if someone does things in a sloppy manner.'[38]

Exercise Honest Optimism

Ratan describes himself as 'a bit of an optimist'. He is a believer 'in evolution rather than revolution', and he never feels that something can't be done. 'It may take a little time and may not happen quite the way you wanted it to, but I always feel that it can be done. I am a moderate risk-taker, but I am not risk-averse, nor am I a gambler. If I believe in something, I pursue it vigorously.'[39]

His personal satisfaction is bound up in the achievements of the Tata companies. 'What would really make me happy is to have people say that we are a group that provides value for money and that our customer sensitivity is very high. In other words, I have no desire to strive to necessarily be No. 1 in size. But being No. 1 in quality and No. 1 as a corporation in its human and business practices would be really great.'

In terms of his own legacy, he would like to be remembered as 'someone who succeeded in an environment of change, and upheld the value system and the ethical standards that our group was built on'. His great 'satisfaction' in having presided over corporate growth 'without crossing the line that distinguishes ethical practice from some of the things we see around us today'.[40] If this sounds like a relatively modest aspiration for a life's work, it is in fact, both modest and highly ambitious. To consistently succeed as leader of both an unabashedly capitalist enterprise and an uncompromisingly ethical enterprise is, in the context of the history of business, an extraordinary achievement. But under Ratan Tata, it really happened.

5

Challenges

Ups and downs in life are very important to keep us going, because a straight line even in an ECG means we are not alive.

—Ratan Tata

The ultimate measure of a man is not where he stands in moments of comfort and convenience, but where he stands at times of challenge and controversy.

—Martin Luther King, Jr

No 150-year-old enterprise employing some 660,800 people and operating as a conglomerate of more than 100 companies can properly be called simple. Yet the core ethical principle of this venerable giant can be distilled to a single concept: 'There is no right way to do the wrong thing.' The Tata companies have always operated from a compelling moral base, and the morality of sound ethics is rarely easy, but almost always simple in that it is unambiguous.

The Ethical Challenge

Yet simplicity can be complicated, even in matters of morality. A case-in-point is the mandate, often reiterated by Ratan, that no Tata company will ever pay a bribe. This position by no means represents a modern Tata reform. On the contrary, it is an affirmation of a policy that began with Jamsetji Tata at the very start of the enterprise. The policy, however, was put to the test during the early years of Ratan's leadership, which coincided with the liberalization of the Indian economy under the administration of Prime Minister P.V. Narasimha Rao and the finance minister, Dr Manmohan Singh, which began on 21 June 1991 and lasted through the first five years of Ratan's chairmanship of Tata Sons. Rao took steps to loosen the so-called Licence Raj, the arcane system of regulations, red tape, permits and licences that had been required to conduct business in India ever since Independence in 1947 and through 1990.

It must be noted that the prime minister's efforts were only partially successful, and Ratan's attempts to advance strategic growth and expansion with new businesses were still repeatedly thwarted by government regulation, particularly in core and infrastructure-related sectors.

The customary way out of this lingering bureaucratic morass was bribery, a practice institutionalized in Indian government. Ratan's predecessor as Tata Sons chairman, J.R.D. Tata, had steadfastly refused to make illicit payments for licences, and Ratan embraced this ethical tradition, reasoning that a culture of bribery was lawless and therefore bad for Indian business in general, bad for Tata in particular and, most important of all, bad for India.

There is, after all, no right way to do the wrong thing. Nevertheless, the Tata Group paid a high price for doing the right thing. They saw licences for entry into new markets and for major plant construction repeatedly go to competitors. Coming, as they did, at the outset of his chairmanship, these competitive defeats were not only hard on Tata, they were hard on Ratan. Yet, despite the competitive cost, he stood firm on his principles, which had been JRD's as well as Jamsetji's. They were in fact Tata principles, and Ratan's faith was that his company's example of ethics would, in the longer term, bring an end to the prevailing culture of corruption. The great challenge was to stay the course, even when others ponied up and pulled ahead. But Ratan believed that the great strength of the Tata enterprise, which had sustained it well into the company's second century, was a consistent refusal to sacrifice long-term goals and timeless ethical principles for short-term gains.

To be sure, it is tempting to tell yourself that the well-being of your business demands cutting some moral corners.

Ratan believes that he owes his grandmother, Lady Navajbai, much of his grounding in 'values and ethics . . . many, many things that she lived by came from her to my brother, Jimmy, and me'. Lady Navajbai was responsible for essential elements of Ratan's early personal history. He explained that she had a role in stiffening his moral spine, which made it easier for him to confront a basic challenge posed by Tata company history.

'Jamsetji Tata took a national view,' he explained to Indian business historian Gita Piramal, 'and so, inevitably, we were in basic industries and infrastructure. After Independence, these became the natural domain of the public sector.' As such, Tata businesses tended to be those most stringently subject to the Licence Raj. 'Through the '60s and '70s, excessive government controls . . . deprived Tatas of growth. Our passenger car proposals were rejected. TISCO [today, Tata Steel] was not allowed to expand in the manner that was needed, and its entry into special steels was thwarted.'[1] During the administration of Prime Minister Indira Gandhi (1980–84), a prospective deal between TELCO (today Tata Motors Limited) and Honda was lost in a tangle of government red tape. A series of Tata proposals—to build a refinery, petrochemical complex and fertilizer plant—were throttled. The expansion of Tata Power was repeatedly thwarted.

Indeed, the Indira Gandhi administration denied virtually every Tata application for expansion.

The succession of Rajiv Gandhi as prime minister after the assassination of his mother on 31 October 1984, offered reason to hope that the Licence Raj would at last be forced to release its death grip on Indian commerce. Whereas relations between Indira Gandhi and JRD had been chilly, those between Rajiv and Ratan were much warmer. Their cordial relationship was based neither on politics nor bribes, but on common interests, not the least of which was a love of flying.

The two men met in 1980, years before Rajiv became prime minister. 'We had dinner together and I was struck by his politeness and sincerity,' Ratan recalled. 'After that we did not meet for a few years. When he took over as Prime Minister, I was very much excited by the things he was saying, the freshness with which he was looking at economic and political issues. I felt here was a prime minister who was a man of our times.' Ratan met with him at this time 'not to ask for anything but just to express my happiness and excitement at the new direction he was charting out for the country. I was once again struck by his decency, sincerity and forthrightness.'[2]

When asked who among India's leaders had most impressed him, Ratan reflected a moment[3]—'Who impressed me the most?'— and then answered that he 'was closest to Rajiv Gandhi. I really believed that he could change India.' Ratan's admiration was obviously reciprocated, and Gita Piramal observes, 'Their friendship and mutual admiration brought about a major change in the [Tata] group's attitude towards the government, and vice versa.'[4]

In September 1986, Rajiv Gandhi appointed Ratan chairman of Air India, which JRD had founded (as Tata Airlines) in 1932, had been partially nationalized in 1948 (when the newly independent India acquired a 49 per cent stake), and wholly nationalized in 1953 (when the government acquired a majority stake via the Air Corporations Act). JRD, for whom the airline was a cherished enterprise, was devastated by what he called nationalization 'through the back door'.

It had been the work of India's prime minister, Jawaharlal Nehru, a socialist who distrusted private enterprise. 'I can only deplore,' JRD wrote to Nehru, 'that so vital a step should have been taken without giving us a proper hearing.' Even so, JRD served as the chairman of the nationalized airline until 1977, when Prime Minister Morarji Desai removed him.[5]

Ratan's appointment as Air India's chairman by Rajiv Gandhi came as a surprise. 'I read about my appointment in the papers!' Ratan told the Piramal.[6] But the nationalized airline was always burdened by debt. JRD had told Prime Minister Nehru bluntly that India's nationalized companies—the so-called public-sector units (PSUs)—needed to make a profit. This provoked a sharp retort from the prime minister: 'Never talk to me about the word profit; it is a dirty word.' As of this writing (June 2017), Air India's debt is some Rs 50,000 crore, and there is the prospect that the airline's history will come full circle if the Tata Group decides to risk the purchase of a controlling share.[7]

During the administration of Rajiv Gandhi, there evolved between Ratan and the prime minister 'a close advisory relationship'. Ratan recalls in particular his great pleasure in working for the science and technology ministry, including as a member 'of a technology mission to the US, where the effort was to set up a venture capital company in that country which could buy high-tech companies'. 'The mode would roughly be what the Tatas did with Elxsi,'[8] a Silicon Valley minicomputer manufacturer, processor designer and operating system creator founded in 1979, partly with Tata Group funding.

Tata project applications that had been smothered for years under red tape were now being approved. 'Suddenly our success rate in getting licences has changed dramatically.'[9]

Tragically, the liberalization of the Licence Raj did not survive the assassination of Rajiv Gandhi on 2 December 1989.

Meeting the apparently straightforward moral challenge of refusing to do the wrong thing even when your rivals had no such scruples, proved difficult and costly. But it was worth it in the long run, as the Tata companies emerged into the present era of liberalization with their ethics and ethical reputation intact. Tata's reputation for trustworthiness was especially valuable as the company ventured into global enterprises.

Fast forward to 31 October 2014, when Epic Systems Corporation, a US-based healthcare software company, brought suit against TCS and Tata America International Corporation for what the suit described as 'brazenly stealing' Epic's 'trade secrets, confidential information, documents and data'. The case is complex, but the allegation amounted to this: The US-managed care consortium Kaiser Permanente, an Epic customer, hired TCS to provide consulting services relating to the Epic software. In 2014, a 'whistle-blower' told Epic that TCS employees were accessing Epic's digital network and downloading data used to develop TCS software that competes with Epic's. In its suit, Epic charged that the downloads represented some twenty years of its development work, including documents detailing the operation of Epic's source code. In April 2016, the jury agreed, handing down a judgement against TCS of $240 million in compensatory damages and $700 million in punitive damages.[10] The award was subsequently reduced to $720 million in total and is under appeal.[11]

Ratan has said[12] that he 'finds it difficult to believe that TCS' would 'wilfully' do what Epic alleged, but he was also very straightforward about the essential problem a leader of even the most ethically committed company faces. 'I've always been cognizant of the fact that we have some 600,000 employees, and I can't vouch for the integrity of every single employee.'

'But you do take such pride in Tata ethics . . .'

'Yes,' Ratan agreed.

'Would you have been in favour of giving Epic $100 million to go away?' he was asked.

'No,' Ratan replied without hesitation.

'So, hypothetically, let's say you know you're in the right, but you can make the problem go away by paying someone a settlement fee rather than going to court and risking a far greater loss. You would not settle? On principle, you would not settle?'

'If it is a business settlement, I have no problem with that. If it's a settlement in the sense of being a pay-out or receipt or something of that kind, I wouldn't have a problem doing that. If I were not sure about what had happened in a case, I would, taking care not to compromise anybody's position, go and meet with the other party. I would sit down and talk. The result might end up being a settlement, but it wouldn't be paying $100 million to get someone off our back. The only settlement I would accept is one in which we and the other party did something *together* to resolve the dispute. This isn't always possible, but it is the only ethical alternative to defending yourself in court.'

The Family Challenge

Refusing to do the wrong thing is simple to understand, but, as Ratan points out, it is not always simple to execute. Another seemingly simple aspect of leadership within Tata is the company's reputation as a family business. For the sake of argument, let's assume that the vast Tata conglomerate really is, at its foundation, just a family business.

We all come from, live with and produce families, and we know—or we soon learn—that families are actually far more complicated than any business. Ratan was a child of divorce, and that makes the inherent complexity of family life even harder to cope with. Although Ratan and his brother Jimmy were, after the divorce, largely raised by their grandmother Lady Navajbai, they also lived with their father, who, Ratan has said,[13] 'took us along with him wherever—you know, when he would go to the beach house or have his friends visit—people much older than we were. We had very few friends who were our age or in school, because we were never allowed to go off and do our own thing. We were always dragged as an appendage to my father's entourage.'

When asked how his father handled his divorce, Ratan said, 'Well, my father certainly was very bitter, and that reflected itself in everything we did. Jimmy and I were not allowed to visit my mother as often as we might like.'

Despite a calm demeanour, Ratan was asked, 'Obviously there must have been a lot of turmoil in your first twenty years of life— emotional turmoil. That must have been a challenge.'

'Oh, there were emotions,' he replied. 'There was loneliness. There is—that's why I said I owe a great deal to my grandmother, because she filled all those gaps, and she gave so much of herself to us. Still, I grew up in a household where the mention of my mother's name was almost taboo.'

'So, living in America during your college years must have given you some space and some perspective—your own perspective, finally.'

'Getting to the US and being away from the family, I had the opportunity of taking my own positions on what had happened. I understood that my not having a good relationship with my mother was because it was not allowed.'

Ratan's American experience also taught him something else, he made clear: 'Americans have less of an issue about who you are, whose son you are and how much family money you have. In the US, I learned, you can be successful from the street, if you have the capability.'

While it is clear that Ratan has a healthy perspective on what the family does and does not mean to the business, he does not minimize the fact that the main promoter company in the group is called Tata Sons, and there are and have always been strong elements of a family business throughout the Tata enterprises. Still, it is evident that in very significant ways, Tata is not a family business at all. For one thing, thirty of the companies in the group are publicly held, and, taken together, the conglomerate is both incredibly enormous and diverse. In his 1983 Strategic Plan (Chapter 3), Ratan pointed out that the Tata Group's holdings in the companies were becoming dangerously diluted, which meant that the group's control over the direction of the companies was slipping.

He recommended to the directors that the group increase its holdings and that cross-holdings between companies, including Tata Sons, be permitted. Ratan's objective was to prevent an outside takeover of any of the constituent Tata companies. He was anxious to hold the conglomerate—and its founding ethos—together. At this point, JRD apparently shared neither Ratan's anxiety nor his opinion in this, and the idea of increasing the group's holdings in the Tata companies was tabled.

Thirteen months after he succeeded JRD as chairman of Tata Sons, Ratan returned to the substance of his 1983 Strategic Plan. This time, it was JRD who proposed, at an April 1992 board meeting, a massive Rs 220 million rights issue in favour of the group. This and other aspects of the revival of Ratan's plan, as well as some directors' objections to it, leaked to the *Economic Times*. The paper published, on 8 May 1992, a scathing editorial charging that the 'new game plan of Messrs JRD and Ratan Tata to convert the Tata group from a loosely-held confederacy to a centralized family business affects lakhs of small shareholders and government institutions'.[14]

Ratan responded sharply to the editorial, pointing out that he had 'always acted in the best interests of [Tata] shareholders and there has never been an abuse of shareholders' funds to acquire or gain control of Tata companies through Tata Sons.' He took 'very strong exception to such motives being ascribed to Mr JRD Tata and myself'. Even more, Ratan objected to the statement that there is a move to convert the Tata Group 'from a loosely-held confederacy to a centralized family business'. Tata Sons has been, and continues to be, professionally managed by a board of directors and not by 'family members as alleged by you'. Ratan next shifted from a personal to an ethical defence, charging that the editorial's 'allegations and insinuations' were 'an effort to discredit the values and philosophy on which the House of Tata has been built. It shall always be my endeavour to uphold the Tata values and philosophy.'[15]

In this response to the editorial, Ratan refuted the very notion that the Tata enterprise is or can be a simple family business. Not only had it long been 'professionally managed', its allegiance was also *never* to a family, but to certain 'values and philosophy'. This was an obvious allusion to the philanthropic purposes that motivated Jamsetji's sons, Ratanji and Dorabji, to put charity at the core of the company. It was not family control over the Tata companies that Ratan was struggling to maintain. It was central control by Tata Sons, an entity 66 per cent owned by the Tata Trusts. Ratan was concerned to save the philanthropic, socially responsible heart and soul of the enterprise.

The Leadership Challenge

Even if the Tata companies were not rooted in philanthropy, even if they had been intended solely as a means of enriching a single family and its descendants, today's conglomerate would still not be a 'simple' family business. As discussed in Chapter 2, the Tatas are both a family and a family business. While it is something of a glib and formulaic oversimplification, there is nevertheless value in Gita Piramal's observation that the Tatas, in effect, 'reconstructed' themselves, adopting and cobbling 'together people to make a family', so that they can 'promote talent rather than blood relations' to create the leadership of the business.[16]

The downfall of many family businesses comes when the enterprise is treated first and foremost as a means of employing family members, regardless of their abilities. The Tatas have never been content to play this genetic lottery. They have, of course, drawn on the family for leaders, but they have assiduously educated, chosen, groomed and prepared some among them. In 1991, the Tata companies appeared to have senior leadership candidates in the wings who did not share the Tata surname. And it was therefore something of a surprise when Ratan was chosen that year as chairman of Tata Sons.

Review where he was coming from. After living in the United States from 1955 to 1962, acquiring a degree in architecture from Cornell University, he responded immediately to the desire of his grandmother, Lady Navajbai, to see him. He left Los Angeles, where he was living, to return to India to be with his grandmother, whose health was failing badly. Eventually, he chose to stay in India and join TELCO (today Tata Motors) and TISCO (today's Tata Steel Ltd) where, in each case, he worked on the shop floor of several departments of those companies. In 1971, JRD assigned him as CEO (a position at the time called director-in-charge) of NELCO, the National Radio and Electronics Company, a maker of consumer electronics.

It was a desperately ailing firm, which Ratan managed to turn around—at least temporarily. His 'reward' for this achievement, in 1977, was the leadership of Central India Textiles, which had been founded by Jamsetji Tata as Empress Mills and was now— as NELCO had been—seriously ailing. Again, Ratan largely managed to turn it around—at least as far as he could without securing from Tata leadership the additional investment he called for. In 1982, Dr Dattatray Samant, a politician and labour leader better known as Dutta Samant or, simply, Doctorsaheb, led between 200,000 and 300,000 textile workers on strike in Mumbai. Among the mills that shut down during this year-long action was Empress. Without the required investments, it closed permanently in 1986.

Anyone who manages a business sooner or later learns the acute pain of being saddled with an adverse situation that is not their fault but is nevertheless their problem. This was precisely the challenge confronting Ratan in his first two leadership assignments. Given the reins of one sick company and then another, he performed very well—certainly much better than anyone had a right to expect— and yet the fate of the two companies was widely seen as one failure after the other. For Ratan, the challenge was to resist buying into this narrative of failure by keeping hold of the facts, the numbers. Given two sick companies, he made them better. By the numbers, he had not failed at all. That the recovery of these companies was not permitted to become permanent was not his fault.

Nevertheless, from the perspective of outside observers, the failures were his problems. And when Ratan was finally tapped to succeed JRD as chairman of Tata Sons in 1991, the choice seemed at best surprising and at worst blatant nepotism. The truth was that, despite his surname, Ratan appeared to be a relative outsider, at least compared to the likes of Darbari Seth of Tata Tea and Tata Chemicals; Ajit Kerkar of the Taj Group of hotels; Nani Palkhivala, prominent on the boards of several Tata companies; and—above all—Russi Mody, chairman of TISCO (Tata Steel). Among these leaders, Mody's claim to the throne seemed virtually unassailable, and, as we saw in Chapter 3, his effort to ascend to the chairmanship became a bitter sparring match that attracted national attention in India.

Ratan was keenly aware that his appointment as group chairman hardly enjoyed universal support. He admitted, 'There were some in the Old Guard who didn't simply resent my being named chairman, they just didn't want to see any change at all. I realized that they had to go. There were others who were supportive of change, and I encouraged them to stay with the organization, which they did—until they either retired or died.'

Could their minds have been changed? He reflected, 'It was not me as a person the hard cases were resisting. It was change. There were a few directors who were dug in against change, and there were others who were not positively against change, but they did think that everything was fine as it was. They didn't so much resist change as they simply believed there was no need for it, period. They felt that there was no need to change any business transactions, and no need to enter into any new businesses.'

So, his first challenge was not so much overcoming resistance to him as a person, as it was overcoming resistance to questioning the status quo.

Ratan agreed that it wasn't really about him. Nevertheless, in an interview at the time of his retirement as chairman in December 2012, he was asked whether, when he was appointed, he doubted his 'ability to provide the group with the kind of leadership it required'. He demurred slightly, responding that it was 'a difficult question to answer'. But then he continued by quite precisely defining the challenge that met him when he was named to succeed JRD:

'JRD Tata . . . had . . . had around him a team of senior managers, all of them people of substantial standing in their respective spheres. They had high public acceptance and were people with proven track records. While they may have acceded to his wish that I take over the chairmanship—and this happened suddenly—I must confess that I did not feel any sense of joyousness on their part, because some of them had aspirations to have that job themselves.'[17]

The insiders—Seth, Kerkar, Palkhivala and Mody—were often referred to as 'the satraps', using the term applied to the provincial governors of the ancient Persian empire. The four men were powerful and much-esteemed. Entrusted with great responsibility, they were also accustomed to great deference. Whatever else they were, Ratan saw them as holdovers from an authoritarian style of Indian management that was rapidly becoming outmoded and was certainly unsuited to doing business on a global stage. He defined the challenge of asserting his own authority as a perilous high-wire act:

> It was a period of tightrope walking: on the one hand, trying to continue the cordial relationships I had with them, not as chairman of the group but as one of their colleagues, and at the same time trying not to avoid taking the decisions on changes that I felt were needed to be taken. The first five years of my being chairman were spent in negotiating and in trying, as diplomatically as I could, to achieve what I was convinced had to be achieved, in some instances to the annoyance and even anger of some of these stalwarts.[18]

There was also lurking in the background, the young, up-and-coming Nusli Wadia. Born in Mumbai in 1944, he is the son of Neville and Dina Wadia, the grandson of Dina's father, Muhammad Ali Jinnah, founder of Pakistan, and the godson of JRD. Deemed one of India's wealthiest businessmen, he is chairman of the Wadia Group. So why did JRD select Ratan to succeed him instead of one of the satraps or his own the high-profile, high-flying Nusli Wadia? There were at least two reasons.

First, JRD was well aware that the initial leadership assignments he had given Ratan were trials by fire. Ratan had been deliberately assigned to lead two companies expected to fail. Nevertheless, he managed to turn them around, at least as far as he was permitted to do so. JRD surely appreciated this display of character and competence, but he did not judge it as sufficient reason to promote Ratan ahead of the satraps and even ahead of his own godson.

Gita Piramal is quite likely correct in her view that JRD saw in Ratan someone who, like himself, understood and cherished the Tata 'ethos'. Piramal believes that, having witnessed the unseemly 'scramble among the company chiefs to succeed him and the unpleasant innuendos that surface[d]', JRD urgently wanted to appoint 'someone who understood the Tata ethos . . . and . . . he thought Ratan Tata was someone who could uphold this ethos'.[19]

Ratan's reverence for Tata ethical traditions proved extraordinarily valuable. Navigating the myriad challenges that face any corporate leader requires, first and last, a powerful moral compass. What JRD may or may not have also hoped to accomplish by nominating a relative outsider was introducing into the top level of Tata leadership someone young enough and independent enough to 'change Tata to help it keep pace with a changing India'. At the start of an era of economic liberalization, Indian companies were 'suddenly in a new environment' and 'could not keep operating under the old market rules, the old certainties'.[20]

Taking Charge

Russi Mody was unseated as chairman of TISCO when he accused, in the pages of *The Hindu*, Ratan (deputy chairman of the company) and Jamshed J. Irani (managing director) of so badly mismanaging TISCO that its share prices plummeted. An emergency meeting of the TISCO board was called on

19 April 1993. Ratan calmly defined what he called the 'main issue', which was, he pointed out, 'that a chairman either agrees with his management's policies, or he leaves the board'.[21] Thus Russi Mody became the first satrap to fall. Next came Dabari Seth, who retired in 1995, and Ajit Kerkar two years later, after Ratan successfully installed a policy setting the retirement age for senior executives at sixty-five and at seventy for directors. Nani Palkhivala became the last of the satraps to leave, when he retired in 1997 for reasons of ill health.

The end of the reign of the satraps brought a finish to the high-wire act, which had been running for some five years. During this time, Ratan's challenge had been to lead his company into the new era with sufficient patience to avoid alienating the satraps and their loyalists, yet with just enough alacrity to prevent competing firms from leaving Tata in the dust. Once free from old-guard constraints, however, Ratan directed his attention to reinvigorating both TISCO and TELCO.

Renamed Tata Steel, TISCO became highly competitive as one of the world's lowest-cost steel makers. TELCO, founded in 1945 as the Tata Engineering and Locomotive Company, turned out its first commercial motor vehicle in 1954 but did not enter the passenger vehicle market until 1991, with the three-door Tata Sierra SUV. In 1998, the company launched the Tata Indica, not only Tata Motors' first passenger car, but India's first indigenously developed passenger car. This paved the way for the Tata Nano, launched with a price of Rs 1 lakh—$1500—making it an affordable alternative to two-wheeled transportation.

The transformation of TISCO made Tata Steel a major supplier of the commodity, and the transformation of TELCO made Tata Motors a player in the global automotive market. These changes are representative of the Tata Group under Ratan's leadership. A great but rather stodgy Indian manufacturer was at last emerging as a global brand, with a greater emphasis on consumer goods. In this, the company was being positioned to take full advantage of India's liberalization of commerce and industry.

The challenges included reshaping aspects of Tata's brand identity both internally, within the company, and externally, in the marketplace. Part of Ratan's programme involved making major new investments in expansion, while other aspects of the effort required difficult decisions to exit some long-held business areas, such as cosmetics, textiles and cement. At the same time, Ratan led the group into emerging growth areas that included telecommunications and software, as well as finance and retail. A particularly dynamic growth company was TCS, which had been founded in 1968 with a very limited brief in computing services. By the 1980s, TCS became active in software development, and, under Ratan's watch as Tata Sons' chairman, it evolved into a multinational IT service provider as well as a consulting and business solutions company.

But whose decision was it to completely change the direction of TCS from being a low-end operational company, going all the way up the full consulting food chain?[22]

'I would say the change started with F.C. Kohli in his last few years as the CEO of TCS, but it was accelerated by Ramadorai,' says Ratan.

He was CEO of TCS from 1996 to 2009 and its vice-chairman until 2014. Under Ramadorai's leadership, the company grew from $400 million in revenue and about 6000 employees to one of the world's largest software and services companies, with some 160,429 employees on board, revenues of $4.5 billion, and profits of $1.2 billion.[23] As spectacular as this was, Ratan shared, 'Chandra has taken it to new heights.' That is Natarajan Chandrasekaran, who became the new chairman of the board of Tata Sons in January 2017. He had taken over from Ramadorai in 2009 as CEO of TCS, having been COO of the company. In 2016, TCS reported $16.54 billion in revenue and $3.7 billion in profit,[24] making TCS Tata's most profitable company.

If this was the new status quo, most business leaders would have grabbed it and held on to it for dear life. Ratan, however, is convinced that 'TCS needs to reinvent itself now because the outsource IT business is going to be controlled by machines as machine learning advances and analytics advances. Predictive kind of work is going to be mechanized, and traditional IT services are going to diminish. Human-executed IT services are going to yield to automation.'

Asked what he would you do if he were Chandra today, Ratan's answer was immediate and succinct: 'I would invest in analytics today, and apply it to get me out of the analytics and predictive business so that I could transition into the coming digital future.'

Even as Ratan led a revolution in what Tata makes and what markets Tata serves, he led a campaign of persuasion to convince the group companies to pay a royalty to Tata Sons for both the direct and indirect use of the Tata brand name. In parallel, the global growth in product and service offerings and the higher valuation of the brand name greatly increased the recognition and the value of the Tata brand. This in turn contributed to centralizing the conglomerate, a structural feature of the Tata Group enhanced by Ratan's push to increase the ownership stake of the promoter firms. In this way, the integrity of the brand was strengthened by ensuring that the group companies would not be vulnerable to takeover.

With the departure of the satraps, Ratan significantly enlarged his scope of action. Nevertheless, achieving balance between the independence of the constituent Tata companies and their identification with the group brand remained a dynamic challenge. Cohesion and brand identity are critical, but so too is maintaining a manageable scale that is conducive to agility and innovation.

The Challenge of Growth

Balancing growth with an identity established more than a century and a half ago poses a challenge of its own. Organic growth is the expansion of an enterprise by increasing output, expanding customer bases and innovating new products. Each of these three modes of organic growth is important, especially with respect to building a company's brand. But inorganic growth—growth through mergers and acquisitions—can be a faster, more immediately productive form of growth, adding to capacity while simultaneously reducing competition—and doing both in the short-term. Beyond the financial costs of inorganic growth, however, is the risk of diluting the brand. The risk is real enough, and it is heightened by the possibility of anxiety and resistance within the company, which may have an impact on loyalty and morale.

During the mid-1990s, Tata Tea attempted to acquire British teabag giant Tetley. The attempt failed, but Ratan was not ready to abandon the idea of a synergistic acquisition. Tata Tea was a brand powerhouse in India and the Middle East, but it had not penetrated UK, European, US and Canadian markets, which were the domain of Tetley. In 2000, a second attempt to acquire Tetley was successful, and Tata made not only its first major acquisition but also the largest acquisition, at that time, of a non-Indian company by an Indian company.

With the purchase, Tata Tea became the world's second-largest tea company, gaining a presence in more than forty countries. Yet Tata Tea did not simply gulp down Tetley Tea and Tetley's other recognized brands. Under Ratan, Tata developed a policy of applying the Tata brand name wherever it made sense to do so. But in cases where a valuable brand was already well established, as in the instance of Tetley, Tata generally used the existing brand name. Good business was not a matter of corporate ego.

In 2005, Tata Tea acquired the US brand Good Earth, retaining its brand name as well. The following year, 2006, it added Eight O'Clock, a popular American coffee brand, as well as Jemča, the leading tea brand in the Czech Republic, and 33 per cent of Joekels Tea (which became a subsidiary in 2011), one of the largest-selling South African tea brands. Grand, a Russian coffee brand, was acquired in 2009, and in 2010, Tata Tea was renamed Tata Global Beverages, an umbrella under which the Tata Tea brand was now gathered, along with all the other tea, coffee and beverage brands, which came to include Australia's Map Coffee in 2014.

While the acquisition of Tetley by Tata Tea remains the Tata Group's biggest acquisition in the consumer packaged goods category, the group's largest overall acquisition to date is that of the Anglo-Dutch steel maker, Corus Group Plc in 2007. Despite its $13.1 billion final price tag—which had been bid up in competition with a rival suitor, Brazilian steel company Companhia Siderúrgica Nacional (CSN)—Ratan called the acquisition a defining moment for the company.[25]

It increased Tata Steel's capacity threefold, taking it from a middle-tier regional producer to global status as the fifth-largest steel company in the world. This globalization was in sync with Ratan's overall strategy throughout his chairmanship, and, in the case of steel, it made very specific sense. Extending the global reach of Tata Steel spread the risks inherent in producing and marketing what is, after all, a commodity. Besides, the economic outlook was heady and hopeful when the Corus acquisition was completed in April 2007. Moreover, outward foreign direct investment was increasingly common during this period, and hesitation to seize the main chance looked to be fatal in the long run.

As Ratan explained to Tata's Christabelle Noronha in a 2003 interview, 'I think risk is a necessary part of business philosophy. You can be risk-averse and take no risks, in which case you will have a certain trajectory in terms of your growth. Or you can, while being prudent, take greater risk in order to grow faster.' Tata's global competitors were taking those high-velocity acquisition routes to growth. Could Tata afford to be overtaken? In the past, the answer would have been yes. 'I think, as a group, we were risk averse and we hardly grew because either it was not safe or no one else had done it before,' Ratan told Noronha. 'I view risk as an ability to be where no one has been before. I view risk to be an issue of thinking big, something we did not do previously. We did everything in small increments so we always lagged behind.'[26]

Still, the fact remained that the price Tata paid for Corus in 2007 was about a third higher than what had been quoted in 2006. The stock market did not respond well to this, but Ratan stood firm. 'The market is taking both a short-term view and a harsh view,' he told a Rediff interviewer. 'We often damn a company when it makes a loss in a single year. We applaud a company when it makes an extraordinary profit. But the life of a corporation is much longer than a single year.' Ratan admitted that many thought the acquisition 'was an audacious move . . . an Indian company making a bid for a European company much larger in size. I believe that this will be the first step in ensuring that the Indian industry can in fact go outside the shore of India in an international market place and in fact acquaint itself as a global player.'[27]

But, alas, the movie that now unspooled was far from a happy one. In 2008, the Great Recession gripped the global economy, and optimistic handshaking turned to anguished hand-wringing. In FY 2009, Tata Steel's net profit fell 60 per cent, and then the company made a loss of Rs 2009 crore (about $321 million) in FY 2010. Profits rebounded in FY 2011, declined the following year, and then plummeted in FY 2013 by Rs 7058 crore (about $1130 million). FY 2014 saw a rebound, FY 2015 another loss and FY 2016 a slight profit. The company's share price on the BSE fell by 2016 to half what it had been in 2007–08, while its debt rose 40 per cent from FY 2008 to FY 2016.[28] In 2009/2010, the steel plant in Teesside, England, was shuttered and sold. Other UK plants were mothballed, and in 2016, the company's Long Products division was sold to Greybull Capital for a single pound, with the buyer assuming all assets as well as liabilities.

Dare to Fail

Against the backdrop of the Great Recession, the acquisition of Corus Steel was almost universally regarded as a failure and a defeat. Ratan faced the reality of the disappointment, and he certainly accepted responsibility for the failure of the acquisition to produce the quick fruits of rapid growth he and others had anticipated. Yet he did not see it as a defeat because he did not regard failure as synonymous with defeat.

Since the early 1960s, when he was a student at Cornell, Ratan counted John F. Kennedy among his idols. He is fond of quoting the thirty-fifth American president: 'Those who dare to fail miserably can achieve greatly.'[29] Ratan believes that, far from signalling defeat, failure is a key to long-term innovation, growth and success. He has even called 'failure . . . a gold mine',[30] and in 2006 championed the introduction of the Tata InnoVista programme to 'celebrate the successes and struggles of innovation'. The purpose of the programme, which awards prizes for innovation, is to 'capture innovations of Tata companies and to instil self-confidence among Tata managers'. It is also to 'recognise innovators and encourage innovations in companies', to 'share and learn the levers used by companies to identify and execute innovation projects', and to 'build a culture of appropriate risk-taking'.[31]

As conceived in 2006, Tata InnoVista emphasized promising and successful innovations; however, the very next year, 2007, a new category was added to the programme. It is called Dare to Try—but might just as well have been called Dare to Fail. It 'recognises sincere and audacious attempts to create a major innovation that failed to get the desired results. The idea is to encourage the culture of 'risk taking', perseverance and sharing openly. This award is a celebration of the spirit that propels individuals and teams to try and innovate and is a reward for the risk-taking capability that is necessary for path-breaking innovation.

The setbacks suffered as a result of the Corus acquisition did not discourage Ratan from leading the charge to acquire JLR from Ford Motor Company for $2.3 billion in June 2008. But it took nerves of steel when that acquisition nearly died aborning. Ratan related how Tata had 'bought Jaguar Land Rover with our money from Tata Motors, and then the downturn came in Europe'—the great global meltdown that had begun in the US during 2007–08.

'The banks,' Ratan recalled, 'most of them, were taken over by the British government. The Royal Bank of Scotland was our largest banker in JLR. It and every other bank we went to was under the control of the British government, and all our sources of working capital suddenly disappeared. All these banks said, "Sorry, we have to cancel our commitment to you." So, I went to Prime Minister Gordon Brown, who put me on to Peter Mandelson, Britain's Secretary of State. Basically, he went around the bend, up and down the street, and into the alleys and out, but finally did nothing except say to me, "You are an Indian company. You should go to the banks in India." But the jobs are British! I reminded him. "*Well*," he politely responded, "I'm very sorry. But we think you're an Indian company. You need to go to an Indian bank!"

'So, I went to an Indian bank,' Ratan continued, 'the State Bank of India. But I was afraid that the Indian banking system would not be so willing to stand the risk of supporting a company in the UK, not in such rough economic times. To my surprise and relief, thanks to its chairman, the State Bank of India decided to stand with us. They provided the working capital, and we made it through.'

Despite being a risky loan, Tata persevered.

'We didn't default,' says Ratan. 'We paid back everything we owed. Our relationship with the bank has been very good, and, in hindsight, I believe that, had the decision gone another way, Tata Motors would have been in jeopardy—and the State Bank of India would have lost much more than it gained.'

Since then, the JLR profit picture has been a huge success. From a loss of £376 million in FY 2009, JLR has shown a profit in every year, reaching £2614 million in FY 2015.[32] As the *New York Times* commented in 2012, four years after the acquisition, 'the well-known but somewhat faded British brands are regaining some of their lost lustre, racking up big sales from Shanghai to London'. It is, the paper observed, a success that 'has stunned analysts and investors, many of whom had said that Tata Motors, the Indian auto company, was making an expensive mistake when it acquired JLR'.

Analysts were forced to admit that Tata accomplished 'what few companies from emerging markets have been able to do— turn around and successfully run a troubled Western company.' Earlier, many pundits 'speculated that . . . Ratan Tata . . . had become too enamoured of buying global brands', but the fact was that Ratan understood two key features of the acquisition. First, he saw the great value of the JLR brands—and, consequently, did not impose the Tata brand on them. Instead, he adopted a 'hands-off' attitude, leaving the day-to-day management of the company to executives headquartered in England. Second, he recognized that what Tata brought to promotion of the JLR brands was Tata's own financial reserves and (to use a word an anonymous executive from a rival car company applied) its 'staying power'.[33]

Since this chapter was written, JLR has been faced with the challenges of Brexit. That, along with the general move away from diesel, caused the company to have its biggest one-year loss ever. Fortunately, JLR seems to have turned the corner and is predicting a return to profitability next quarter.

The sequential but overlapping journey from the Corus to JLR acquisition, from disappointment to success, encompasses the most formidable challenge a leader of a major enterprise faces. It is to take the bold risks that achieve long-term, strategic growth while, if necessary, absorbing short-term reversals and failures without reframing your mindset, attitude and vision in terms of defeat. The burden of guiding an old, storied, iconic enterprise—an enterprise with which the very pride and identity of a great nation are intimately bound—is heavy indeed. The temptation is to lead retrospectively, with an eye turned towards the past. While Ratan is strongly rooted in the founding values of the Tata companies, he resists the retrospective lure, the temptation to indulge reverence for the status quo. Instead, he invests in the future. For the leader of India's largest and most consequential company, the core challenge is in the sheer magnitude of the stakes.

6

How to Handle Even the Worst of Times

'Peter, you could not ever think of coming up with a compensation plan that would ensure the sort of devotion the Taj employees demonstrated. That was when I really appreciated that, at Tata, we had created something unique and very special. In a strange way, the worst of my time as chairman helped me appreciate just how special a company we had created.'

—Ratan Tata, in conversation with Peter Casey

The preceding chapter was about challenges—meeting them, dealing with them, and, wherever possible, converting them into opportunities. To understand the Tata enterprise and Ratan Tata's role in it, it is important that we understand how the company has historically dealt with adversity and challenge.

At the beginning, in the days of Jamsetji Tata and his sons, it was the challenge of building a company that would be instrumental in bringing India into a new industrial century and civilization. For the company in the 20th and 21st centuries, the challenges have been economic, regulatory, political and technological. But sometimes, they have been, in the starkest sense, existential. In our age, corporate leaders have been confronted by catastrophes natural and manmade. Few leaders have had to confront any event more horrific than the 2008 terrorist attack on the Taj Mahal Palace Hotel. Thirty-three persons lost their lives in this assault on this icon of both Tata and India. Most formative events, most events that reveal about a leader, come relatively early in a career. Ratan was seventy-one when the terrorists attacked this most tangible incarnation of Jamsetji's legacy to the company and the nation. Managing challenges is a business leader's stock in trade. Having to lead the enterprise and its people through unspeakable cataclysm is unexpected, but when the need arises, it cannot be evaded.

The Taj Mahal Palace is very special in many ways. It was the only one of Jamsetji Tata's grand plans that he actually saw to fruition in his lifetime. The other three, building an institute of technology, a steel mill and a hydroelectric dam, would all happen after his death in 1904. The Taj Hotel's 'magic' did not originate in the basalt and domes of its exuberant architecture, but in the mind, imagination and soul of Jamsetji Tata. It is a monument to his passion for India and to his faith in his nation's future.

Ask Ratan what the absolute low and high points of his chairmanship were and he will undoubtedly cite the Taj Mahal attack. Without hesitation, said Ratan, 'Obviously, the 2008 terrorist attack on the Taj Mahal was the low point.' He continued, however, to say something that suggested it was also among the high points. 'Ironically, even though it took a long time for the full extent of the tragedy to become clear, it also, in a strange way, made me realize that at Tata, we really had created something very special.'

He explained that, on the night of the attack, there were 1100 guests and 500 Tata employees in the hotel. The workers were, by and large, the main breadwinners for their families. When the attack started—the hand grenades started going off, the fires started and mass panic began taking over—the staff remained at their stations and worked tirelessly to try to evacuate the guests to safety. Ratan recalls how some of the employees formed human chains to guide the guests out through the dark chaos. Not a single employee deserted their post. This vision is in stark contrast to what would likely have happened at any other fancy hotel anywhere else in the world. Anywhere else, it would have been 'every man for himself and let's get to hell out of here!'

As for Ratan, he always looked beyond himself and even beyond the Tata organization. While the Taj lay under siege, he was on the phone with the chief minister, trying to convince him that the attack on his hotel was not an isolated incident but a concerted attack on all Mumbai. Ratan's persistence finally convinced the chief minister to dispatch India's Special Forces, its anti-terrorist commandos.

Ratan went to the Taj and stayed there until every last guest and employee had been accounted for. He pledged to completely restore the hotel and to look after the families of those killed or injured. Reflecting on the challenge of that day, he said, 'You could not ever think of coming up with a compensation plan that would ensure the sort of devotion the Taj employees demonstrated. That was when I really appreciated that, at Tata, we had created something unique and very special. In a strange way, the worst of my time as chairman helped me appreciate just how special a company we had created.'

Front Bay, Back Bay

The southern portion of Mumbai thrusts out from the west coast of India and into the Arabian Sea. The Front Bay, also called Bombay Harbour, is on the east side of this picturesque urban peninsula. It is here that the Taj Mahal Palace overlooks the Gateway to India. On the west side of the peninsula is the much larger Back Bay. Very often, in life as in business, threats do not enter by the front door, but steal in by way of the back.

The morning of 26 November 2008 had been a bright Wednesday at the height of wedding season. Mumbai was in a festive mood and nowhere more than among the crowds at the Gateway of India, a grand celebratory landmark built between 1913–24, a few steps from the Taj. A writer for *Vanity Fair* set the scene on that Wednesday: 'Politicians and socialites and bankers from Saudi Arabia packed the rooms of the hotel . . . That night there would be a wedding in the Crystal Room for the scion of a prominent textile family, a private dinner for the board of the Hindustan Unilever company, and a banquet with European dignitaries in the Rendezvous Room. Drivers, waiters, chefs, pool boys and driveway attendants in towering turbans were starting their day. Because of riots in the region the month before, a police detail had been dispatched from the hotel to other parts of the state. The banquet staff was relieved that the VIPs would not have to go through the onerous security checks.'[1]

Come Wednesday evening, ten jihadists, trained in a remote mountain camp in Muzaffarabad, Pakistan, by Lashkar-e-Taiba ('Army of the Good'), a terrorist organization funded by Osama bin Laden, made their way across the Back Bay waters in a motorized yellow dinghy. They headed towards the chain of lights—the 'Queen's Necklace'—that adorns the graceful curve of Marine Drive along the bay's edge.

At the south end of Back Bay, where the curve of the Queen's Necklace breaks abruptly into an almost-rectangular harbour, is a place called Badhwar Park. It is misleadingly named. Amid the wealth of this part of Mumbai, Badhwar Park is an 'unregulated fishermen's colony', close to the Oberoi and Trident hotels that front the Back Bay at Nariman Point and a short distance from the Taj on the Front Bay. At Macchimar Nagar in an area called Cuffe Parade, six of the terrorists disembarked at 8.10 p.m. local time. They carried several large rucksacks, each of which held AK-47 assault rifles and ammunition, hand grenades and handguns. Noticing that they did not appear to be fishermen, a few curious locals asked them about their occupation.

Students. They said they were *students.*

When the other four men landed a bit farther along the shore, Marathi-speaking fishermen wanted to know who they were. *Mind your own business*, they replied, and then the four split into groups of two.[2]

The Opening Attacks

On the Colaba Causeway is the Leopold Café, which has been popular with foreigners since it was established in 1879. It is less than a block from the Taj. A security guard at a Benetton store opposite the Leopold saw two of the men get out of a yellow cab, lugging their rucksacks. It was 9.43 when the guard heard one of them say, 'Come on, brother, let's say Bismillah [In the name of God the Most Gracious, the Most Merciful].' With that, they each pulled out an AK-47 from their rucksacks, entered the Leopold, hurled a grenade into the café and began 'drilling rounds into the crowd inside the café and out in the street'.[3] They killed ten people and injured many more. Elsewhere nearby, bombs in two taxis exploded, killing five and wounding fifteen.

In the meantime, at 9.20, two other terrorists stormed the Chhatrapati Shivaji Terminus (CST) railroad station, hurled grenades and opened fire with their AK-47s, killing fifty-two and wounding 109. At 10.30, they entered the nearby Cama Hospital. Alert and heroic hospital staff locked down all rooms on the wards, thereby saving their patients' lives. A gunfight erupted between the terrorists and police. One attacker was killed, the other captured.

Under Siege

It was now approximately 11 p.m. Four of the terrorists entered the Taj and began shooting. News organizations, including NDTV,

The Evening Standard and the BBC, have all compiled timelines of what happened next.[4]

By 11.30, no more than six police officers are inside the hotel. By midnight, large numbers of Mumbai police begin to surround it. At 1 a.m. on 27 November, a blast erupts in the central dome of the Taj, igniting a major fire. An hour and a half later, Indian army troops arrive in two trucks and storm the lobby as fire spreads across the hotel's top floor. At three, the fire brigade arrives amid shooting heard inside the lobby and elsewhere in the main building. Braving both the flames and the gunfire, firefighters use their ladders to rescue more than 200 people by 4 a.m. Within a half-hour—by 4.30—the attackers have all moved from the 'heritage' building—the Palace—to the adjacent modern Tower (opened in 1973).

At about 5 a.m., commandos and bomb squad personnel arrive as the police become more aggressive in attempting to end the siege. At 6.30, swarms of security forces storm the hotel, liberating some people between 8 and 9 a.m. But at 10.30, a new gun battle erupts. Approximately fifty hostages are evacuated by about noon, yet an unknown number of terrorists and hostages remain in the hotel. At 4.30 p.m., the attackers set fire to a fourth-floor room. More commandos are summoned and enter the Taj at 7.20 in the evening.

The siege carries over to a third day. At 2.53 p.m. on 28 November, authorities recover six bodies, but during the next hour, ten grenades detonate within the building. More bodies are recovered at approximately 4 in the afternoon. At 7.30, more explosions and gunfire are heard. An hour later, commandos report that only one attacker remains in the hotel.

On 29 November, between 3.40 and 4.10 in the morning, five more explosions detonate. It is Day Four of the siege. At 7.30 that morning, the fire rages on the first floor and black smoke billows through the second. Gunshots are too numerous to count. It is a full-on gun battle between one terrorist and many officers. It ends after a half-hour, when commandos declare the hotel under government control.[5]

Standing Up

One hundred sixty-six people were killed and more than 300 injured in the November 2008 terrorist attacks against Mumbai. Thirty-three of those killed died at the Taj.[6] Timelines and numbers are grim records, to be sure, but they convey remarkably little of the kinetic reality of the violent, chaotic human events. Asked to recount the Battle of Waterloo in detail, a victorious Duke of Wellington famously remarked, 'The history of a battle, is not unlike the history of a ball. Some individuals may recollect all the little events of which the great result is the battle won or lost, but no individual can recollect the order in which, or the exact moment at which, they occurred, which makes all the difference as to their value or importance . . .'[7] It is even more difficult to make sense of the chaos that is terrorism, but this is precisely the task that Ratan Tata was faced with during the attack.

As Cathy Scott-Clark and Adrian Levy document in their *The Siege: 68 Hours Inside the Taj Hotel*, Indian security forces warned hotel security and the Tata organization that their intelligence indicated the possibility of an attack. In an interview with CNN's Fareed Zakaria on 29 November 2008, Ratan said that hotel security was increased in response to the warnings but was disliked by the hotel guests.

'They planned everything . . . I believe the first thing they did, they shot a sniffer dog and his handler. They went through the kitchen.'[8] In the weeks before the attacks, Vishwas Nangre Patil, deputy commissioner of police for Mumbai's Zone 1, had urged the Taj to implement very extensive security measures. 'Patil wished to create a fortress, while the Taj needed to remain a theatre.'[9] In the aftermath of the attacks, Ratan conceded that the hotel could have done more, but that no practical measures could have stopped the attacks, which challenged even government security forces.

Ratan took care to avoid passing the responsibility on to any person or agency. 'We were getting the cooperation that they [police and emergency workers] could give us, but the [city's security] infrastructure was woefully poor,' he explained to Zakaria. He cited the fact that it took three hours for firefighters to simply get water to the hotel after a blaze broke out in the oldest part of the building. It was a matter of inadequate infrastructure. And it was a matter of inadequate equipment. 'We had people who died being shot through bulletproof vests,' Ratan pointed out. He told Zakaria that the attacks revealed a need for law enforcement to develop infrastructure for crisis management.[10]

If anything, Ratan was being too generous. The truth is that Mumbai police and security forces were underequipped, understaffed and unprepared. Of the terrorists, joint commissioner of police Rakesh Maria would later say, 'They learn and adapt. We [the civil authorities] stagnate, squabble and steal from one another.' As the attacks began, Maria wondered if the city's total security forces of 40,000, tasked with protecting a population of 13 million, could even begin to get a grip on the crisis. Forty thousand for 13 million was well below what the United Nations recommended as a minimum ratio.[11] At the start of the attack, all Maria could do was observe the horror and make calls to his field commanders: 'Go in, go in! Keep them pinned down!' The state-police commissioner, A.N. Roy, stood across the street from the Taj. He shouted into his cell phone, 'Why aren't they going in?' Maria later commented, 'We were a city at war,' yet police and security officials were often at odds with one another and indecisive. Mumbai's deputy police commissioner for Zone 1, Vishwas Patil, dialled his boss, the commissioner. 'It's do or die!'

he shouted into his phone, only to have his superior respond: 'The army is on its way. Wait for backup!'[12] As in terrorist attacks elsewhere, especially the US, the wait-for-backup approach would prove heartbreaking.

'We've been very complacent,' Ratan said, 'because we've really not had this kind of terrorism inflicted upon us [before] . . . We should go to the best place possible to get expertise.' He called on Indians to unite behind the goal of preventing another such attack. 'Rather than have us succumb to this kind of terror, what [the attack] has done is given us a resolve that nobody can do this to us [again] . . . We're indignant, but we're not scared. If there's a view that this has pulled us down, I think it will unite the country that much more.' He had faith that this would happen because, he told Fareed Zakaria, the hotel's 'general manager lost his whole family in one of the fires in the building. I went up to him today and I told him how sorry I was, and he said, "Sir, we are going to beat this. We are going to build this Taj back into what it was. We're standing with you. We will not let this event take us down." And that is the feeling that [Taj employees] have, and I have a feeling that that's pretty much echoed throughout the country.'[13]

Ratan said, 'The attack on the Taj was in magnitude bigger than anything else I'd ever face, but, by that time, I discovered I was strong enough to face a situation like that, which, earlier, I may not have been able to do. If the attack on the Taj had come before the violent TELCO strike,' he confessed candidly, 'I don't know what would have happened. Fortunately, the strike had taught me a lot. It matured me, fast. Perhaps it gave me the confidence to deal with the crisis at the Taj in 2008. Could I have done it without the experience of the strike? It is difficult to tell.' He continued: 'You have to keep remembering that your business is also the business of your customer and your stakeholder. You have to live up to his expectation, and you have to be a person who produces the products and services your customer can trust.

At the Taj, this included doing whatever was necessary to protect your guests.'

It is in fact an attitude that Ratan shares with his employees and they with him. Raymond Bickson, chief executive of Taj Hotels Resorts and Palaces, told the *New York Times* about how he encountered Karambir Singh Kang, the Taj general manager Ratan mentioned in his interview with Fareed Zakaria. 'I happened to be in the hotel having dinner with friends when I got word that some sort of gang war shooting was taking place in our main lobby,' Bickson related. 'Excusing myself to investigate, I came out of the Tower elevators into the lobby and saw Karambir Singh Kang . . . From the other side of the lobby, which was covered with shattered glass, he shouted at me to go back upstairs, which I did, but then was stranded there for the next twelve hours until I was rescued . . . Later, Karambir found out he'd lost his wife, Neeti, and both their sons, Uday and Samar, fourteen and five. They were trapped by fire in a suite where they were staying, while Karambir worked tirelessly to save other guests. Even after hearing of their deaths, he would have kept on working were it not for our insisting he take time off to be with his parents and other close family. His bravery is typical of almost all the hotel's associates on duty that night and of the others who came in when they heard what was happening.'[14]

Karambir was at another Taj property when he heard about the attacks. He left for the besieged hotel instantly. As recounted in a 2011 *Harvard Business Review* story, 'He took charge at the Taj Mumbai the moment he arrived, supervising the evacuation of guests and coordinating the efforts of firefighters amid the chaos. His wife and two young children were in a sixth-floor suite, where the general manager traditionally lives. Kang thought they would be safe, but when he realized that the terrorists were on the upper floors, he tried to get to his family. It was impossible. By midnight the sixth floor was in flames, and there was no hope of anyone's surviving. Kang led the rescue efforts until noon the next day. Only then did he call his parents to tell them that the terrorists had killed his wife and children. His father, a retired general, told him, 'Son, do your duty. Do not desert your post." Kang replied, "If it [the hotel] goes down, I will be the last man out."'[15]

I often give talks, to students and other groups, about business ethics. One of my examples contrasts how the employees of the Taj, including Karambir Singh Kang, responded to a deadly terrorist attack with how the captain of the Italian cruise ship *Costa Concordia* responded when he ran his ship aground off Isola del Giglio on the Tuscan coast in 2012. Whereas Kang pledged to be the 'last man out', Captain Francesco Schettino was pretty much the first man off the ship—and many of his crew followed, leaving the passengers to fend for themselves.

Are both Karambir Singh Kang and Ratan Tata stubborn? That may be, but the better word to describe them both is *courageous*. Even this, however, is not quite right. Like stubbornness, courage is a trait. In the case of those who work for the Tata companies, courage and heroism are less personal traits than they are values of the organization—values that percolate from the top to every lower layer of the company.

On the evening the attacks began, Harish Manwani, chairman, and Nitin Paranjpe, CEO, of Hindustan Unilever, were hosting a dinner at the Taj. The company's 'directors, senior executives, and their spouses were bidding farewell to Patrick Cescau, the CEO, and welcoming Paul Polman, the CEO-elect'. The banquet was serviced by about thirty-five Taj employees under the direction of twenty-year-old banquet manager Mallika Jagad. At about 9.30, as the main course was being served, she and her staff heard what they initially assumed was fireworks from a nearby wedding. In short order, however, they realized it was the sound of gunshots. Jagad ordered the doors locked and the lights turned off. She instructed everyone to lie down quietly under tables and asked them not to use their cell phones. She further directed that husbands and wives separate 'to reduce the risk to families'. For the rest of the night, this group stayed together, listening to the rampage outside. The staff, guests later reported, were incredibly calm. They quietly circulated throughout the night, offering water and 'asking people if they needed anything else'.[16]

Come morning, a fire broke out in the hallway outside. Jagad and her staff organized an evacuation through the windows—guests first, staff second, their manager last of all. Firefighters used their ladders to facilitate the escape.

'It was my responsibility . . . I may have been the youngest person in the room,' Jagad later told one the authors of the *Harvard Business Review* article, 'but I was still doing my job.'[17]

Elsewhere in the hotel, others also did their jobs. The staff of Wasabi, the hotel's Japanese restaurant, received a warning call from the hotel operator: terrorists with assault rifles were headed their way. 'Forty-eight-year-old Thomas Varghese, the senior waiter at Wasabi, immediately instructed his fifty-odd guests to crouch under tables, and he directed employees to form a human cordon around them.' After four hours, security men asked Varghese if he could get the guests out of the hotel. 'He decided to use a spiral staircase near the restaurant to evacuate the customers first and then the hotel staff. The thirty-year Taj veteran insisted that he would be the last man to leave, but he never did get out. The terrorists gunned him down as he reached the bottom of the staircase.'[18]

The *Harvard Business Review* authors write, '[After the attack] guests were overwhelmed by employees' dedication to duty, their desire to protect guests without regard to personal safety and their quick thinking. Restaurant and banquet staff rushed people to safe locations such as kitchens and basements. Telephone operators stayed at their posts, alerting guests to lock doors and not step out. Kitchen staff formed human shields to protect guests during evacuation attempts. As many as eleven Taj Mumbai employees—a third of the hotel's casualties—laid down their lives while helping between 1200 and 1500 guests escape.'[19]

'Our studies show that the Taj employees' actions weren't prescribed in manuals; no official policies or procedures existed for an event such as 26/11.' Yet the actions came from somewhere. The *Harvard Business Review* authors believed 'that the unusual hiring, training and incentive systems of the Taj Group—which operates 108 hotels in 12 countries—have combined to create an organizational culture in which employees are willing to do almost anything for guests.'[20] Ratan was justifiably proud of the group's employees as they came through the attacks, but I get the impression that he was not at all surprised. They understand each other. Like him, they are steeped in the company's founding values.

The instances of Taj personnel going above and beyond what anyone anywhere would expect from a mere hotel employee are too numerous to cover comprehensively. Ratan understood that, while they did indeed go above and beyond, they did so because of the values they had imbibed working for what is by any measure an extraordinary company. The fact is that none of them thought of themselves as 'mere hotel employees'. They were what Tata leadership told them they were—indispensable to Tata as guardians of the company's guests.

Adil Irani, manager of the hotel's Aquarius poolside restaurant, put his life on the line by shepherding his guests to whatever safety he could find for them. He kept trying to identify some means of escape—*for them*. At one point, he deliberately drew the attention of a gunman away from his guests. 'As he ran, his shoes slapping against the marble floor, he felt a rush of bullets flying past, nicking his clothes and kicking up plaster and marble.'[21]

Taj general manager Karambir Kang made the difficult decision to 'get the switchboard girls back to their desks and call everyone'.[22] It put these young women in danger, he knew, but it was essential to saving many more lives. The switchboard operators alerted managers and guests everywhere, passing on critical instructions. These young people became a bulwark against chaos.

Amit Peshave, the twenty-seven-year-old manager of Shamiana, the twenty-four-hour Taj coffee shop, 'spotted a gunman hovering outside'. The man looked no older than him and was wearing a grey long-sleeved T-shirt over a black polo neck, with a bulky blue cricket bag thrown over one shoulder. Amit could see writing on it: 'Changing the Tide'. Amit had to make a life-or-death decision: run or stay. With his guests relying on him—he counted thirty-one—he stayed. Amit urged them to get underneath the tables, then he quietly gathered them together with the intention of leading them into two private salons at the rear of the restaurant. Holing up there, he figured, would at least buy them all some time.

As he herded his guests, he turned around and 'saw Rehmatullah, the head waiter, emerge from the kitchen, carrying a plate of biryani'. He called out to warn him, but the gunman 'spotted him too and squeezed off a burst, catching the old man in the chest, throwing him on to his back, the tray clattering to the floor, rice flying around the room'. For good measure, he then bowled a grenade towards the buffet counter, just as Amit's assistant manager emerged to see what the noise was about. 'Run,' Amit screamed, as the grenade detonated, shattering the crystal chandeliers, throwing the room into jagged and choking darkness as his assistant rolled out of the way.[23]

'Amit scanned the restaurant and his eyes came to rest on the "dead door". Normally, a live band played in front, but he remembered it led into the gardens beside the pool terrace. Hidden in the shrubbery was the hotel's transformer room, from where another door opened out into Merry Weather Road: a secret door to the street.' He made his way to the closed door and 'kicked and kicked' it until it gave way, sending him 'tumbling out into the night air. He was out. For a few seconds he lay there, looking up at the stars. "Amit, save yourself. Run for your life." Could he live with that decision? He thought of his parents in Pune, philanthropic GPs [general practitioner physicians] who often worked for nothing. No, he could not live with that decision. He went back inside.'[24] Eventually, Amit was able to lead his guests through the 'secret' exit and to safety.

Coffee shop manager Amit Peshave was not widely known outside of the Taj, but Hemant Oberoi, the fifty-three-year-old grand executive chef of the Taj Mahal Palace Hotel, was India's most celebrated culinary artist and achieved an international reputation, taking 'Taj's gourmet business to exponential heights, introducing trendsetting cuisines and restaurants that served world-class fare' and, on a daily basis, overseeing 1241 chefs.[25]

When his hotel was attacked, Oberoi marshalled what came to be called 'his Kitchen Brigade to form a human chain to escort guests out of the hotel'. The Brigade was conveying some thirty guests out when the terrorists opened fire on them. Nitin Minocha, senior sous-chef of the hotel's Golden Dragon restaurant, turned and saw fellow chef Vijay Banga shot in the back. Both men went down. Minocha would recover; Banga was dead. Under fire, the Brigade began to break apart, 'the human tunnel disintegrating, staff and guests bolting for their lives'. At that point Thomas Varghese, a Syrian Christian who was headwaiter at the Wasabi Japanese restaurant, deliberately dashed into the line of the fire, 'shepherding strays away from the gunmen'. When a fatal bullet found Varghese, Rajan Kamble, a Taj engineer, 'came out of nowhere and blocked the gunman's path for a few vital seconds before taking a [lethal] round in his back'. Another colleague, Taj chef Raghu Deora, also leapt into the line of fire, but survived. 'Kitchen Brigade' chefs Hemant Talim, Boris Rego, Kaizad

Kamdin and Zaheen Mateen all gave their lives in defence of their colleagues and guests.[26]

Rising Again

The siege of the Taj Mahal Palace Hotel was still under way (despite mistaken claims from the police that it had ended) when Ratan made a public statement:

> 'The terrible wanton attacks last night on innocent people and the destruction of prominent landmarks in India deserve to be universally condemned. My sympathies and condolences go out to all those who have suffered, been injured, and those who have lost their loved ones in this terrible act of hatred and destruction.
>
> We cannot replace the lives that have been lost and we will never forget the terrifying events of last night, but we must stand together, shoulder to shoulder as citizens of India, and rebuild what has been destroyed. We must show that we cannot be disabled or destroyed, but that such [a] heinous act will only make us stronger. It is important that we do not allow divisive forces to weaken us. We need to overcome these forces as one strong unified nation.'[27]

Years later, Ratan would call 'the terrorist attack in Mumbai, in which many lost their lives . . . a life changing moment for me. For six months, my voice was breaking and I could not speak clearly . . . Every evening, I used to go to hospitals, visit families. For three days, I saw that there was nobody to even pay their bills. It was after that that we formed a trust to rehabilitate all known and unknown victims.'[28]

Ratan did not hesitate to pledge that the Taj would be completely restored and set the goal of reopening the relatively intact Tower within a month. However, as Raymond Bickson, chief executive of the Taj Hotels Resorts and Palaces, wrote in the *New York Times,* 'While reopening the hotel was important, our first response was to our fellow employees and guests. Within twenty-four hours of the attack, we set up five outreach centers for our associates and guests. We had fifteen experts in post-trauma counselling talking with people individually and in small groups. It's a process that will continue for quite some time.'

Bickson noted, '[The families] of the 15 Taj employees who died will be paid their deceased's salaries for the rest of their lives, as well as all medical benefits and education for those up to age 24. In addition, the Taj Hotels have set up a trust to provide immediate relief to all families of those who were killed, whether from the general public, the security forces, and employees of the Taj or of other establishments affected by the terrorists.'[29]

Mr R.K. Krishnakumar, deputy chairman of the Indian Hotels, proposed that the Taj should undertake a broader responsibility for the victims. Ratan immediately agreed, and the Taj Public Service Welfare Trust was set up to provide relief not just for Taj victims but for 'hundreds of terror victims [in the Mumbai attacks] who have been forgotten in officialdom and time'. The trust provides such aid as monthly sustenance, loans and set-up endowments to help terror victims rebuild their lives. While the trust furnishes monthly payments to families who have lost their breadwinner and reimburses victims' medical expenses, its chief aim is for the long term, to help survivors build sustainable livelihoods. After discovering that 'the school and college dropout levels among kin of terror victims had gone up', the trust began financing educational expenses. As Deepak S. Bhatia, director of the trust, explained, 'We are in touch with hundreds of schools across the country. We have spoken to the principals directly and assured them that the fees will be paid by us. This year we have already paid for the entire year.'

Wherever necessary, the trust pays for tutors, for 'books, uniforms, shoes, umbrellas, geometry boxes, pencils, pens, school bag and anything else [children] need for school'. The trust has paid for rehabilitation and prosthetics and has intervened to find suitable employment for those with disabling injuries. Vocational training is also a focus, with special emphasis on the hospitality industry. 'As of July 2012, 55 aid recipients, mostly the children of 2008 attack victims, were working in Tata hotels.'[30] The Taj employees had cared for guests of the company's hotel, and now Ratan saw to it that Tata cared for the employees. It was the right thing to do.

On Sunday evening, 21 December 2008, Ratan Tata presided over a ceremony dedicating—to 'those who have lost their lives'— the reopening of the Tower wing of Taj. 'We cannot be knocked down—this is a memorable day and a tribute to those who saved many lives. It gives me a great sense of pride—this is the start of a new era.'[31] Some 1000 people attending this ceremony 'applauded for 15 minutes straight, tears streaming down many faces, as the 540 Taj employees on duty the night of 26/11 strode proudly through the lobby on a red carpet.'[32]

The day before, Ratan had led 'an event for staff only. Spiritual leaders from all major faiths conducted prayers and healing rituals. We read aloud the names of all 1700 of the Taj Mumbai's employees. It took 45 minutes. Just to hear all our names echo in that hall was so reaffirming. It united us in a way that went deeper than the usual team-building programs.'[33]

The international reaction to Ratan's response to the 2008 attack on Mumbai and the Taj was overwhelmingly positive. 'While it has the sympathy of the world,' *Forbes Magazine* senior editor (Asia) Robyn Meredith wrote in a *Forbes* article, 'India could have an Obama moment—one in which a leader, whose personal history epitomises the country's principles, marches forward to unite the country during its very moment of trauma. India has a chance to get it right, but it needs a strong, credible leader to step up . . . As an American, I don't get a vote in India, but if I did, mine would go to Ratan Tata.' Online, Meredith asked, 'Should there not be a way to involve him in government at the highest level? A fractured India would benefit immeasurably from his acumen, his managerial skills, and his very obvious—but always constructive patriotism.'[34]

Yet, when asked, 'Would you consider politics?' he answered, 'No, never would.'

Ratan does not evade leadership, but he believes that he can do more as a major Indian business leader than as one more politician. He knows where his talents and his passions are.

On 15 August 2010, India's Independence Day, Ratan led another ceremony, this one celebrating the completed restoration of the Palace portion of the hotel. He garlanded a bust of Jamsetji Tata as staff members cheered and tossed rose petals in the air.

'This flagship property, this venerable Old Lady, is going to reopen in the same glory, the same splendour of more than 100 years,' Ratan said, his voice cracking. He had promised to 'rebuild every inch' of hotel. It turned out to be a project that took twenty-one months at a cost of Rs 1.8 billion (about $27 million), and while the focus was on restoration, there was also 'a complete refurbishing of the hotel's luxurious suites, including the Ravi Shankar Suite, where maestro Shankar taught Beatle George Harrison to play the sitar'.[35]

Leap of Faith

'Restoring the Taj is just part of Tata's challenge' ran the headline of a January 2009 story in *The Spectator*, about how 'rebuilding the terrorist-hit Mumbai hotel will be an easier task than steering Jaguar Land Rover and the steel group Corus through a deep recession'.[36]

'There was not a single person who did not rise to do their duty,' declared R. K. Krishna Kumar, deputy chairman of Indian Hotels. Kumar told the story of how Taj's general manager, Karambir Kang, had supervised the hotel's evacuation even as he could do nothing to help his wife and two sons on the sixth floor. 'This year,' *Spectator* contributor Richard Orange wrote, 'the Tatas will need every drop of that spirit as their group faces what will be one of the most difficult periods in its 140-year history.'

> Returning the charred wreckage of the Taj to its former glory will be a monumental task. But it is nothing next to the challenges faced by Tata Motors and Tata Steel, whose $2.3 billion acquisition of Jaguar Land Rover (JLR), and £6 billion acquisition of the Anglo-Dutch steel group Corus, have left them exposed to acutely crunch-prone elements of British industry.
>
> 'There's going to be a recession in the West—quite a deep one,' concedes Alan Rosling, the sole British director at Tata and the leader of its drive to go international. 'It's going to be tough, and some of our businesses are going to suffer.' Taking Corus and JLR into account, more than 60 per cent of Tata Group's consolidated revenues will come from outside India. Indian Hotels, on the other hand, contributes only about a sixtieth of group revenues.[37]

The Taj is a monument to the vision that created a vast capitalist enterprise dedicated to making lives, and life itself, better. Some see the Taj Mahal as a palace of self-indulgence. But Jamsetji intended it as an enduring symbol of a new India, an India he was helping to bring fully into the family of powerful modern nations. The foundation of his palace was not a utopian fantasy, but the solid faith that an earnest, ethical person of business could do very well by doing great good, and that commerce and industry should be noble undertakings that build civilizations and enrich all lives. Such faith was worth investing in, living for and, if necessary, even dying for. The restoration and rebirth of the Taj, costly though it was, especially in a time of global financial crisis, sent a message throughout the Tata organization and the international business community. It was a testament of faith in the big picture, the long view, the future.

'For now,' Orange wrote in January 2009, 'Ratan Tata and the architects of the plan that bet the group's future so heavily on JLR and Corus can only grit their teeth and hope the two UK companies make it through the next 18 months in good enough shape that the strategy starts to make sense—as it did with Tata Tea's acquisition of Tetley eight years ago.'[38] The Tata ethos of faith makes *hope* a more rational strategy than it would be for any company built exclusively on the motives, assumptions and values of conventional capitalism. The restoration of the Taj, like the acquisition of JLR and Corus, was a leap of faith towards the future. It was neither more nor less than a fresh iteration of the company's founding strategy.

7

Relationships

Nobody can hurt me without my permission.

—*Mahatma Gandhi*

The Dinshaw Connection

There are a great many erroneous stories about the Dinshaw relationship with the Tatas and Wadias. The families were indeed close and were leaders in the Bombay community. The Tatas and the Dinshaws were all well known for their deep Zoroastrian faith and extraordinary philanthropic gestures. Both families donated a lot of their wealth to help establish schools and hospitals. However, the Wadia clan's conversion to Christianity caused some strains in this relationship.

One of the great myths of the Tata narrative is that the Dinshaw family was the bankers of Tata, lenders of the last resort. It was widely reported that the Dinshaws had loaned the Tatas Rs 1 crore on two occasions (in today's money, about $2 billion) back in the 1920s to help keep the company afloat.[1] It was rumoured that the Dinshaws had made their money—an absolute fortune—selling supplies to the British Army during the Second Afghan War (1878–81). That part is indeed true.

Another common misconception, quoted by numerous sources, was that sometime during the 1920s, Edulji Dinshaw converted his loans into 12.5 per cent equity in Tata. However, if you examine the Tata Sons Share Registry, you'll see that the Dinshaws have never held any equity in Tata Sons.[2] They certainly arranged and facilitated many loans that the Tatas required, but they never owned a single share in Tata Sons. None. When Ratanji Dadabhoy (RD) Tata died in 1926, he left his holdings to his eldest son, JRD. JRD, explained to Tata chronicler R.M. Lala, in his book, *Beyond the Last Blue Mountain*, that he felt bad about this and decided to divide it equally between his siblings. Like many a good deed done with the best of intentions, it was a decision that would have major consequences for the Tata business.

To pay back the money that Sir Dorab had lent his father, JRD was forced to sell properties. He told Lala that all that was left was the shares in Tata Sons, which equated to 20 per cent of the company, though the exact percentage has not been confirmed. (See a copy of the share registry in the appendices.)

So How and When Did the SP Group Acquire Shares in Tata Sons?

Pallonji Mistry's father initially acquired shares in the Tata Group in 1967, when he acquired 5.9 per cent from Rodabah Sawhney—shares she had been given to her by her brother, JRD. It is not exactly clear from the registry how she ended up with 5.9 per cent. Presumably, she inherited some shares from Jimmy when he died in a plane crash in his twenties.

The next purchase by the SP Group was in 1969, when, much to JRD's annoyance, Naval sold 4.81 per cent of Tata Sons owned by the Ratanji Tata Trust. This caused much angst between JRD and Naval. Ratan explained that Naval did so without consulting

JRD, who did not approve of the sale but was powerless to stop it. It was Naval's way of showing JRD that whilst he was not the chairman, he still had the ability to impact the all-powerful JRD. Ratan, too, was also opposed to his father selling shares to the Mistrys, but was also not in a position to stop the sale.

The final purchase came in May 1974, when Darab, who by this time had fallen out badly with JRD, sold his 6.68 per cent to the Mistrys. A rights issue in 1996 brought the total holding of the SP Group to the 18.40 per cent that it is today. All in all, a total of Rs 69 crore ($11M). The value of their holding in TCS alone is in excess of $2B. This was confirmed by Venkat, the Manager of Tata Trusts.

In sum, JRD's act of kindness, dividing his shares equally among his siblings, seems to have spectacularly backfired. The results in monetary terms alone are staggering, eye-watering and beyond even the silliest dotcom bonanza.

As the share registry shows, in the decade between 1965 and 1975, the SP Group acquired shares in Tata for approximately $11 million (Rs 69 crore). It is difficult to estimate the value of Tata Sons, as the vast majority of the companies are privately held, but the value of the shares in Tata Consulting Services alone is pegged at least at $2 billion. In addition, SP Group has received over $150 million in dividends as a result of its holdings in TCS.

Overall, the SP holdings across the board in Tata companies has been reported in the *Economic Times* as being worth $15 billion. This is through two companies owned jointly by Cyrus Mistry and his brother Shapoor. Even adjusting for inflation, the $11 million invested by SP Group in Tata Sons has given them a return of at least 300 to 400 times their original investment.

By any gauge, this is a massive return on a relatively small investment. It could be argued that with results like this, Shapoor Pallonji Mistry could put Warren Buffet, the sage of Omaha, to shame when it comes to successful investing.

So, yes, Cyrus was fired, but there is no need to shed any tears. *Forbes* estimates the Mistry family to be worth in excess of $20 billion. Unlike many in India, no one in the Mistry family will miss a meal. Whilst Ratan certainly did not begrudge the incredibly massive returns that the Mistrys have made on their Tata investment, their lack of overall philanthropy has not gone unnoticed.

The Rise and Fall of Cyrus Mistry

Well before he needed to, when he was seventy-three, Ratan made it very clear that he was going to step aside when he was seventy-five. At the time, he suggested to the board that they should start looking for a successor. A selection committee of five people—Mr N.A. Soonawala, Ms Shirin Bharucha, (representing Tata Trusts,) Mr Cyrus Mistry, Mr R.K. Krishna (representing Tata Sons) and Professor Lord Bhattacharyya (Independent)—was empanelled. Ratan declined to join the panel lest his presence on the committee be perceived as overbearing, and he wanted the committee to arrive at what they felt was the best decision on their own.

After about eighteen months, no internal candidate had been identified. So the committee initiated the long process of looking at external candidates, both in India and overseas. It proved to be difficult to attract international people of prominence to be headquartered in India. Consequently, the search committee's focus returned to possible internal candidates.

The most prominent internal candidate would have been Natarajan Chandrasekaran. However, Chandra, head of TCS, was otherwise engaged, running and transforming the company that was laying all the golden eggs, supplying a disproportionate percentage of the Tata Group's profits. The committee was inclined to keep Chandra where he was, especially since he did not have an obvious successor. To say the least, removing Chandra from the leadership of TCS would have been problematic.

Cyrus Mistry, who had been a director of Tata Sons for approximately six years and was a shareholder in his own right, emerged as a possible candidate. While he had no experience running a large industrial enterprise, he had always been the voice of moderation in Tata Sons board meetings and was seen to be very balanced in the views he expressed. He had run his family business seemingly well and was a graduate of Imperial College in London and London Business School.

Board member N.A. Soonawala was asked, 'Did you ever get the impression that Cyrus was actually angling for the job?' His reply was interesting. 'No,' he began, 'no, not at the time, but he always had very astute questions that questioned some of the other candidates' suitability.'

After some length, the decision was made to offer Cyrus the position, subject to various well-defined conditions—all of which he accepted. He was appointed deputy chairman in November 2011, to overlap with Ratan for eleven months prior to taking over officially as executive chairman of Tata Sons and Tata Group.

One of the preconditions laid down by the committee, and which was accepted by Cyrus at the time, was that he would dissociate himself from his family business, SP Group, of which he, with his brother Shapoor, was a 50 per cent owner. This mandate was clear from the outset, as laid out in the committee's letter of recommendation to the board of Tata Sons. In it, the selection committee stipulated that, if appointed, Cyrus would 'disassociate himself from activities of the SP Group in a manner satisfactory to the board'. It was based on this important commitment from Cyrus that Ratan, representing the majority shareholder, the trusts, accepted the written recommendation of the selection committee (*see* Appendix A).

That key issue resolved, Ratan was supportive of the committee's decision. He was now keen on handing over the reins. He had frequently remarked, 'I definitely did not want to die in the saddle.' He was looking forward to a year of working alongside Cyrus and effecting a smooth transition.

Accordingly, Ratan undertook to personally introduce and expose Cyrus to the various Tata company heads and external partners. But shortly after the main meetings had occurred, Cyrus took a different approach, and very few meaningful business discussions regarding the Tata Group took place after that first round. Ratan observed that when meetings did take place, they were more often than not discussions on decisions that had already been taken. A requirement of prior consent on certain key issues of Tata Sons was bypassed on more than one occasion, as Cyrus made decisions himself and then returned to the board for formal approval—rubberstamping, as it were. This is likely one source of the discord that emerged between the Tata Sons board and Cyrus.

Bear in mind that the Tata Group had operated for more than 150 years without major controversy. Conflicting issues have always been resolved in a quiet, dignified manner. In 2016, this changed, as the group was forced to take a hard and very controversial decision, which quickly became public, in replacing its chairman, Cyrus Mistry, after just four years in office.

For his part, Cyrus was outraged, claiming to have been completely surprised by his dismissal. Indeed, the very day he was fired, he submitted an open, very detailed, five-page letter to the media alleging various misdeeds and acts of commission and omission by the board—of which he himself had been chairman for four years and during which he had made no critical statements. The letter is so comprehensive and detailed that it hardly seems spontaneous. It is difficult not to assume that it had been prepared in advance and tucked away simply waiting for a date to be attached.

In his letter, Cyrus made statements of gross under-provision, hidden losses and alleged acts of malfeasance that served to spook the stock market, precipitating a loss of 24 per cent in the group's aggregate market capitalization. (The market cap loss has been totally recovered.) As though that were not enough, Cyrus, in his well-timed letter, alleged various illegal acts by the holding company and the philanthropic Trusts that controlled them. After his ouster, he submitted to the various authorities over 2000 documents, seeking their intervention. Again, however, the allegations covered the period under his leadership, during which time he made no such complaints.

Cyrus also levelled charges against individual members of the board of Tata Sons and made accusations of interference and misuse of sensitive information against Ratan and N.A. Soonawala, both trustees of the philanthropic trusts. He lodged all of these allegations with National Company Law Tribunal, established by the government to deal with such disputes.

In July 2018, the National Company Law Tribunal cleared Tata Trusts and Tata Sons of all charges of mismanagement or oppression levied by Cyrus and upheld the provisions of the articles of association of Tata Sons and exercise of rights pursuant to such articles by Tata Trusts. It also upheld the process followed for the removal of Cyrus from the board of Tata Sons. In August 2018, the SP Group filed an appeal before the National Company Law Appellate Tribunal (NCLAT). The NCLAT concluded its hearing in May 2019 and has since then reserved its ruling; that is, the appeal was unsuccessful. During the appellate proceedings, the NCLAT did not stay the operation of the NCLT order.

These events plunged the Tata Group into a raging controversy based on an intense, well-planned media campaign by Cyrus. There were articles in the newspapers and on television virtually every day.[3] The Tata Group, however, announced that it would not 'indulge in a public spat', but would defend its actions before appropriate forums. Over time, the allegations diminished, as there were no business or financial disasters as alleged; the Securities and Exchange Board of India (SEBI) issued a statement clearing Ratan and Mr Soonawala of the allegations that he had accessed or misused sensitive information; and the allegation of interference and disallowance of Cyrus' sphere of leadership was generally seen to be unfounded.[4]

The public was left with questions, however. First: Why, exactly, was Cyrus replaced? Second: Why was his dismissal so rancorous and undignified?

These are good questions.

To the first, there appears to have been ample reason for dismissing Cyrus. He had promised the selection committee and the board that he would dissociate himself from the family business. Ratan drew Cyrus's attention to this on numerous occasions, explaining that his failure to do so was a direct breach of the Tata Code of Conduct and Ethics. Indeed, on 24 September 2013, Ratan handwrote a very thoughtful three-page letter to Cyrus explaining in detail his deep concern about Tata companies giving business to Mistry family businesses, of which Cyrus was a 50 per cent beneficial owner. There appeared to be a conflict of interest, which Tata Sons could not allow.

The nominee directors on the board were firmly of the view that Cyrus was, on more than one occasion, breaching the required approval process laid down in the articles. Cyrus responded that as long as he declared a 'related interest', he was not in breach. Ratan, however, believed strongly that simply declaring a related interest was not sufficient to overcome a conflict. The point was that, apart from exerting influence in getting contracts, Cyrus still received 50 per cent of the profit flowing from the business he concluded between Tata and the Mistry companies.

There were other concerns within the board and the trusts. No action was being taken to address business issues in various operating companies. The group had become too reliant on the profits of TCS and JLR, they believed. Cyrus had surrounded himself with a global executive committee, but very few members of the committee had deep experience in the industries that were the very foundation of Tata. Cyrus had excellent excuses for blaming all problems on legacy issues, rather than addressing problems arising from cyclic markets of certain industries in which the Tata Group was involved. He conveniently forgot that he had been a director when many of the so-called legacy issues were implemented, and he had voted to support them.

During his interview for the chairmanship in 2011, Cyrus was asked whether he would give up his Irish citizenship if selected. According to actual interview notes from that meeting, he was directly asked if he would give up his Irish citizenship, and his response was 'irrespective of whether or not he got the position, this was something he had been considering for some time'. This was not a prerequisite for his elevation to chairman, but it was nevertheless expected that some preference would be given to an Indian National, since Tata is the largest company in India and the founder was fiercely patriotic. Six years later, Cyrus is still an Irishman.

There might have been more. In 2016, under Cyrus's chairmanship, Tata Motors embarked on a plan to raise Rs 3000 crore (nearly USD 419 million) in capital through non-convertible debentures (NCDs), adding to Rs 15,887.25 crore (nearly USD 2.4 billion) in borrowings, which included Rs 5550 crore (about USD 834 million) in NCDs. The problem? Tata Motors had not secured prior board approval. To save face, the board approved the massive transaction retroactively. Cyrus also failed to fully inform the board when he directed Tata Power's purchase of Welspun Renewables Energy for Rs 9249 crore (USD 1.4 billion) on 12 June 2016, without consulting Tata Trusts, the major shareholder of Tata Sons. Tata's articles of association require the approval of the Tata Sons board for investment above Rs 100 crore.

Another simmering issue arose in regard to a provision of the Tata Sons articles, which required the chairman to generate an annual business plan, to be approved by the firm's major shareholders. Once approved, the Tata Sons management would be free to operate within the plan. The articles also mandated the creation of a five-year strategic plan, which was also to be approved by the major shareholders. The strategic plan was to provide a long-term forecast for the company.

According to Ratan, in the four years of Cyrus Mistry's leadership, no meaningful plans were ever generated, other than a straw-man plan, which was presented to the board in September 2016 and never discussed.

As to the second question, the situation grew rancorous as evidence mounted against Cyrus. Ratan and the board rapidly moved towards the conclusion that Cyrus was not complying with his pledges to the selection committee and to the board of Tata Sons. The general feeling was that simply disclosing that there *was* a relationship was not in keeping with the essence of the Tata Company Code of Ethics. The significant increase in the various contracts given to his family company after he took over as chairman was also seen as a major conflict of interest. It was believed that the only way to resolve this was to sever all business contracts with the Mistry family company so long as Cyrus was the group chairman of Tata Sons.

Cyrus initially refused to agree with such an action, conceding only after Ratan said that the entire matter would have to be disclosed publicly. Even thereafter, however, contracts were committed under the guise of new phases of old contracts or extensions.

More worrying to the board of Tata Sons and the trusts was the developing view that Cyrus's leadership would result in the dismantling of the group and reverting it to a collection of standalone companies. This created the growing impression that Cyrus was acting not like a corporate chairman, but a proprietor. After more than one instance of disregard for the framework that had been agreed to on his selection as chairman, the board decided that it would be in the group's best interest if Cyrus were replaced as chairman of Tata Sons and as a director of the various operating companies on which he sat.

This was not a sudden decision—though from the public perspective, given how private most Tata Sons matters are handled, it may have appeared as one. The various breaches of corporate governance norms were brought to Cyrus's attention on several occasions. These were never corrected. Companies and their major shareholders all over the world have faced occasions where they have had no option but to remove or replace chief executives or chairmen. This is the prerogative of the owners and shareholders of the company. Ultimately, they have the responsibility of evaluating the performance (or lack thereof) of leadership. Typically, a dismissed chairman or CEO, including those who are international figures, simply move on. If they negotiate anything, it is no more or less than the terms of their dismissal.

On the day of the firing, according to Ratan, a nominated director of the Tata Sons board personally communicated to Cyrus the decision, which was to be placed before the Tata Sons board. This advance notice was to give him the option to step down voluntarily and in a dignified manner. He refused, saying 'I'll take this to the board,' presumably in the belief that any such move to oust him by the board would be illegal. At the board meeting, there were two abstainers out of the nine members present, and no dissent on the issue of Cyrus's removal.

In response, Cyrus immediately leaked a five-page letter calling into question Tata Sons' operational policies. It is unusual, even unseemly, for an ousted chief executive or chairman to take to the street in an effort to harm the company he formerly led and in which he was a major shareholder. Cyrus's leaked letter was indeed a strange one. Making allegations of wrongful removal, to demand reinstatement, to a plea for retention of directorship of group company boards, and then a sharp shift in the discussion to issues of governance, interference and oppression of minority rights. Such was the sharply winding course of Cyrus's written complaints, all of them lodged without acknowledging that the group, of which he was now so critical, had been under his leadership. He was on the board for six years, vice-chairman for one and then chairman and CEO for four years. Yet, the day after he was fired, Cyrus claimed that the governance—the very framework he acknowledged, operated under and accepted on his appointment as chairman—was fatally flawed.

In the end, there was no single reason for removing Cyrus Mistry, but an accretion of leadership failings. Of these, three critical leadership lessons emerge:

Lesson 1

A CEO/Chairman must own failure as well as success.

Cyrus frequently blamed his predecessor for the faults and failings of a company he himself now led. When it comes to legacy issues, a leader cannot pass the buck—or at least cannot pass it for long. Typically, an incoming CEO/Chairman has perhaps a year in which blaming the predecessor is defensible. After that, he or she must assume full responsibility. This is especially true in the case of Cyrus, who had been, after all, a board member for six years and vice-chairman for one year before he was appointed to chair the company. He was not an innocent bystander.

Lesson 2

A CEO/Chairman must perform.

During the four years of Cyrus's chairmanship, the performance of the Tata Group was far from outstanding, except for JLR and TCS. Performance is a dimension of success or failure that is objectively quantifiable and beyond argument. It was generally acknowledged that TCS's incredible success was a result of the changes made in the direction of the company whilst it was under the leadership of the CEO, S. Ramadorai, and the board led by Ratan. These changes were then implemented by Chandra and his leadership team. Cyrus was not actively involved in the running of TCS. Likewise, it was generally acknowledged that Ralph Spieth was the architect and responsible for the turnaround of JLR.

Lesson 3

A CEO/Chairman must always communicate closely, frankly and in a timely manner with the major shareholder, continually selling his or her vision for protecting the shareholder's investment.

There was increasing concern when, time and again, learning vital company news was not forthcoming from Cyrus, but from the press and other media. Full and open communication and consultation are key.

8

The Future

What I would like to do is to leave behind a sustainable entity of a set of companies that operate in an exemplary manner in terms of ethics, values and continue what our ancestors left behind.

—*Ratan Tata*

The best way to predict the future is to create it.

—Abraham Lincoln

It took Natarajan Chandrasekaran—Chandra, as he is known by everyone—thirty years to reach the pinnacle of Indian business. So just how does someone who hails from a humble farming background rise to become the chairman of the largest company in India? Chandra credits his father with instilling in him a passion for perseverance, discipline and honesty. His other great mentor was Subramanian Ramadorai, the TCS CEO, managing director and chairman who brought TCS from a 6000-employee company generating $400 million in revenue to a 200,000-employee global company, with more than $6 billion in revenue.

Undoubtedly, Chandra learnt much from his father and from Ramadorai, but anyone who knows Chandra will tell you that the perfection and discipline he says his father instilled in him were not so much instilled as inborn. To be sure, Chandra's father must have encouraged and nurtured these qualities. In the end, however, they are Chandra's and Chandra's alone. He applies both passions—especially the discipline—to everything he does, from the way he runs marathons to the way he runs businesses. It is simply natural for him to do so. It is his nature.

Doing what he says—and doing it invariably—is another thing that sets Chandra apart. Once he makes up his mind, he stays the course.

Chandra as Tata Chairman: The First Days

There was speculation that the reason Chandra had not been considered for the role of Tata Sons chairman was because he had spent his entire Tata career in the consulting space and had no direct experience with the many other industries in which Tata was involved. This is a very superficial view. Through his role as CEO of TCS, Chandra was intimately involved with many of the industries in which Tata is active. Over the years, he has developed close relationships with the CEOs of numerous Fortune 500 companies in major industries, including many Tata competitors. It is a measure of the ethical esteem in which Tata is held that TCS consults with companies Tata competes with. As mentioned earlier, it is far more likely that Chandra was not previously tapped for the Tata Sons chairmanship because there was great reluctance to take him away from the helm of TCS, the jewel in the Tata crown, a key revenue and profit centre he had led so well.

Once appointed, on 21 February 2017, however, Chandra wasted no time. He immediately made several key appointments, including appointing a new CFO and bringing in leading industrial strategists.

Another highly significant decision Chandra made was the divestiture of the Tata Teleservices business to Bharti Airtel. This was hailed as a masterstroke, a win-win deal for both Tata Teleservices and Bharti Airtel, which was able to assume 40 million additional users, while Tata was able to get out of a business that was haemorrhaging cash—yet maintain employment for the Tata personnel.

In his first three months, Chandra transformed or jettisoned a significant loss-making venture. Shortly after the deal was concluded, the Mittal family announced that they were donating a massive Rs 7000 crore to their philanthropic trust.

Perhaps the most exciting announcement, however, was from Tata Motors—the development and launching of the Tata Airpod, a small car that will largely be powered by compressed air. This is a joint venture with the French company MDI.

Arguably the most important decision Chandra and the board of Tata Sons has made was to take Tata Sons from public limited corporate (PLC) status to private limited (PL) status, which happened on 21 September 2017. This decision will significantly reduce the ability of the Mistry family to disrupt the day-to day-running of Tata Sons. Under the articles, if Tata Sons fails to declare a dividend for two years, the preference shareholders will get equal voting rights to the ordinary shareholders. Ratan Tata essentially controls 36 per cent of the preference shares. It is, of course, entirely possible that Tata Sons will not declare a dividend for two years, as Chandra may decide to use the profits to pay down debt. Such a decision would further devalue the Mistry stake.

Article 75 of the articles of association of Tata Sons Ltd gives the company the power to ask shareholders to sell their holdings by passing a special resolution. This rule could potentially be used to force Mistry family firms to exit Tata Sons. Tata Sons holds the veto concerning to whom the shares can be sold.

The important thing to remember is that Tata Sons was a private company when the Mistry's bought their stake holding. They were a minority shareholder then and nothing has changed.

The Future of the Trusts and Corporate Social Responsibility

In 2014, the Indian government implemented the Corporate Social Responsibility (CSR) Tax. This mandated that after April 2014, companies with annual revenues of more than Rs 10 billion (£105 million) must donate 2 per cent of their net profit to charity. Permissible areas of charitable donation include education, poverty, gender equality and hunger. To avoid corruption, the policy requires that CSR activities not be undertaken exclusively for the benefit of employees of the company or their family members.

Perhaps the most significant and profoundly enduring of the dramatic changes Ratan brought to the Tata Group are the modifications in how the Tata Trusts distribute their donations. Instead of simply giving to charities—chiefly non-governmental organizations (NGOs)—as the trusts had been doing, they will henceforth partner with government agencies and other organizations to develop long-term sustainable programmes. This is going to have a profound impact on the contribution that the charities make to the communities in which they operate.

At present, the largest companies in the Tata Group are preparing to channel a significant part of their mandatory charity spend to the Tata Trusts, the group's philanthropic arm and owner. This is in line with Tata Trusts Chairman Ratan's efforts to streamline all social spending into one powerful programme. As of late-autumn 2017, Tata Steel, Tata Motors,

Tata Chemicals, Tata Power, Tata Global Beverages and Indian Hotels were in discussions to determine the nature and extent of their collaboration with Tata Trusts. This is a move that will truly ensure that the trusts and charitable giving will always be at the core of Tata operations. One cannot imagine that this would have happened had Cyrus remained at the helm.

These changes very likely mean that Ratan Tata has ensured that the founding legacy of Jamsetji Tata will continue for another 150 years. The most extraordinary fact concerning this remarkable transformation is not that Ratan made it, but that he did so long after the age when most executives have quietly retired, at the threshold of his life's eighth decade.

As for the future of Jamsetji's legacy, Ratan's half-brother, Noel, has recently been appointed to the board of the Ratanji Tata Trusts, and new rules regarding the tenure and regulation of the trusts have been implemented.

Tata's firing of Cyrus will certainly go down in history as one of the most surprising and sensational exits in corporate history, and yet it shouldn't have been. Tata's preference was surely to quietly usher in a new chairman after years of discussions regarding the appearance of a conflict of interest with the Mistry companies. Ratan's three-page letter outlining his concerns and his belief that a new leader was required was delivered to Cyrus years before he was officially let go. To this day, Ratan has refused to share the contents of the letter, another sign that Tata would have much preferred its internal personnel matters to remain private.

Despite the very public changing of the guard at Tata, the company, Tata Trusts and Indian businesses, as a whole, are better off for having endured the spectacle. Realizing that their activities could become fodder for newspaper headlines as well, many CEOs have become more responsive to their boards and more aware of potential public scrutiny. That has only improved operations and communication. Within the Tata Trusts, changes have been made to its governance. New term limits have been introduced to ensure more frequent turnover of leadership, as well as a mandated retirement age. Companies, in general, were also prompted to look at their own operations for improvement opportunities.

While Tata Sons certainly regrets having to fire Cyrus, the more distance we get from the event, the more clear it becomes that it was the right thing to do at the time. All parties involved emerged from that turbulent time stronger and wiser.

The three leadership lessons the end of Cyrus Mistry's chairmanship have left us are important, but there is one lesson that towers above them. It is how to engage a global crisis. Tata has been through two world wars, the Great Depression and two global pandemics. Tata has survived them all. In its response to the Covid-19 pandemic, it has not merely survived but has perhaps created its finest hour. What drives such results are the fundamental principles of building a business based on sound ethics, a business that gives back to society and makes it stronger.

Jamsetji Tata is remembered as the 'father of Indian industry'— legacy enough for any man. But Jamsetji's vision extended beyond even the incredibly ambitious goal of building Indian independence and self-determination through the economic empowerment brought by industrialization. True, he wanted to lift India up so it could claim a place among the capitalist nations of the West, yet even this hardly touched the limit of his vision. Guided by his understanding of Parsi morality, he did nothing less than lay the foundation of a capitalism radically redefined. In contrast to his Western contemporary Karl Marx, Jamsetji Tata did not want to destroy capitalism but co-opt it. The great spiritual mission of a Parsi is to live in such a way so as to make the lives of others better. As Ratan Tata observed earlier in this book, the difference between Marx and Jamsetji was that 'Marx's vision was to take from the rich to feed the poor. Jamsetji's vision was to make the poor rich'.[1]

By building a business, Jamsetji would not only provide a living for his own progeny and theirs, he would also improve the lives of countless of his countrymen. In part, this would come about by simply providing employment, as any capitalist enterprise does. In much larger part, however, the improvement was achieved by ensuring that a high percentage of the profits generated by his business would go to fund philanthropic enterprises and other projects for the public good. This great plan, a radical business model, evolved and was passed down to Jamsetji's sons, Dorabji and Ratanji. As the company's second chairman (1904–32), Dorabji conveyed the model to the leaders who followed— Nowroji Saklatwala (1932–38), J.R.D. Tata (1938–91) and then Ratan Tata (1991–2012).

All these men had one thing in common: they kept the flame the founder had kindled, they cherished it and they passed it on undiminished. Virtually unique in the modern world, the vast conglomerate that is the Tata Group is led by Tata Sons, a holding company that is in turn held by the philanthropic Tata Trusts. Thus, all that Tata is and does functions ultimately to directly fund the public good in myriad ways.

The extraordinary financial, social and moral structure of the Tata business model is the single greatest lesson of the enterprise, and its leadership has therefore been extraordinary. In the succession of chairmen, only one fumbled with regard to the flame, aiming to lead the company in the direction of a more conventionally narrow concept of capitalism. It was at this point that Ratan Tata set in motion the removal of Cyrus Mistry and briefly reassumed interim chairmanship (2016–17) before the elevation of Natarajan Chandrasekaran—Chandra—to the position.

The struggles, within the business and within the Indian legal system, associated with Cyrus Mistry's removal riveted all of India and, at times, seemed to threaten scandal and cataclysm. But nature has a way of putting the turmoil and toil of even the greatest of enterprises in a new perspective. And sometimes nature's way is unimaginably cruel.

Early in 2020, the global Covid-19 pandemic took India by storm. On 28 March, Ratan Tata, in his capacity as chairman of the Tata Trusts, released the following statement to the press:

> The current situation in India and across the world is of grave concern and needs immediate action. Tata Trusts and the Tata group's companies have in the past risen to the needs of the nation. At this moment, the need of the hour is greater than any other time.
>
> In this exceptionally difficult period, I believe that urgent emergency resources need to be deployed to cope with the needs of fighting the COVID 19 crisis, which is one of the toughest challenges the human race will face.
>
> Today, Tata Trusts continue their pledge to protect and empower all affected communities, and is committing Rs 500 crores for:
>
> - Personal Protective Equipment for the medical personnel on the frontlines
> - Respiratory systems for treating increasing cases
> - Testing kits to increase per capita testing
> - Setting up modular treatment facilities for infected patients
> - Knowledge management and training of health workers and the general public
>
> Tata Trusts, Tata Sons and the Tata group companies are joined by committed local and global partners as well as the government to fight this crisis on a united public health collaboration platform which will strive to reach out to sections that are underprivileged and deprived.[2]

In May, Tata Trusts committed to building four Covid-19-treatment hospitals, two in the state of Maharashtra (with fifty beds in Sangli and 106 beds in Buldhana,) and two in Uttar Pradesh (with 168 beds in Gautam Buddha Nagar and 106 beds in Gonda). The facilities included inpatient and outpatient wings, critical-care capabilities, minor operation theatres, basic pathology and radiology, facilities for dialysis and blood storage and telemedicine units. Prior to these undertakings, Tata had donated huge stocks of personal protective equipment (PPE) kits and had initiated 'a pan-India community outreach to induce adoption of health practices in rural areas to prevent the spread of COVID-19', a project that reached some 21 million people in twenty-one Indian states.[3]

Tata Group chairman, Natarajan Chandrasekaran, issued a statement in July 2020 in which he noted the Trusts' commitment of a staggering 1500 crore to Covid response and relief, while Tata employees on their own 'contributed tens of crores towards various response projects'. Chandra noted that the response of the people of Tata was 'a great demonstration of the value of collaboration' and the 'mindset of 'One Tata'. Indeed, he continued, 'the pandemic has shown the importance of living by our principles'.[4]

Chandra went on to detail how various Tata companies retooled to design and manufacture the needed healthcare and other equipment, provide logistical and other expertise and create digital platforms to support pandemic containment as well telemedicine and other public health initiatives. In addition, 'because extraordinary times require us to do some extraordinary things':

> Over the past few months, fifteen Tata group companies have worked to scale meal and food-grain provision and provide accommodation across the country. The Indian Hotels Company Limited (IHCL) has distributed over two million meals to

healthcare professionals and migrant workers, including to over twenty hospitals in Mumbai, Delhi, Bengaluru, Agra and Coimbatore. The company worked with Tata Trusts to support the Mumbai police with daily meals.

Tata Power, Tata Consumer Products, Tata Chemicals, Tata Motors, Tata Advanced Systems Ltd, Titan and Tata Communications each undertook efforts to keep meals flowing to migrant and frontline workers, and those in need across townships, factory locations and settlements where they are located.

IHCL also opened the doors of its various hotels, including properties like Taj Mahal Palace and Taj Lands End in Mumbai, for medical professionals. These rooms helped doctors and nurses spend less time commuting, thereby lowering the risk of viral transmission. Various Ginger properties across the country have also offered rooms for quarantine purposes.[5]

Through this all, the Tata Group laid off not a single employee, even as other large Indian companies furloughed or otherwise let go legions of workers. Ratan Tata told *Business Standard* on 24 July 2020 that such layoffs were 'a knee-jerk reaction and showed lack of empathy among the top leadership'. 'These are the people that have worked for you,' he said. 'These are the people who have served you all their careers. You send them out to live in the rain. Is that your definition of ethics when you treat your labour force that way?'[6]

This is a remarkably direct line deriving from Jamsetji Tata's philanthropic reinvention of capitalism to the mobilization of 'One Tata' in response to the greatest public health crisis the world has faced in the modern era. The course is unerring, too, from the epiphany Jamsetji had when he visited the Victorian textile mills of England and came to the conclusion that the mills he would build in India had much to learn from the English in everything *except* their owners' inhumane exploitation of labour. *You send them out to live in the rain. Is that your definition of ethics when you treat labour that way?* Ratan's words could have been spoken by Jamsetji Tata himself nearly a century and a half ago.

Where some others did what they could to escape the pandemic, in part, by shuttering their businesses and shedding workers, Tata Trusts and Tata Sons embraced the health crisis as an opportunity to lift up their fellow beings. Moreover, animated by the spirit of the 19th-century founder of the company, Tata also looked forward into the future, boldly and confidently.

The workforce of Tata Steel BSL (TSBSL)—about 25,000-strong—'[each] had to be on site during the pandemic to maintain business continuity', which prompted the company to create a comprehensive safety plan and in fact enabled them to conduct 'a kind of forced experiment in reimagining the company's ways of working under extremely tough circumstances'. This led TSBSL to become 'far more digitally enabled, agile, and innovative', in the process learning 'from the pandemic response to build a foundation for the future'.[7]

From the pandemic itself, Tata discovered a whole new set of skills and resources to use towards that future, including leveraging peer networks to change employee behaviour, adopting digital technology more widely than ever before, embracing the prevailing ambiguity of crisis to become more agile and extensively democratizing innovation. By applying the founder's original vision of values and mission, Tata not only confronted the pandemic but harvested from that confrontation future-facing insights for the creation of ever-more-resilient enterprises.

Tata has not merely survived, it has advanced, it has served, it has saved lives and, as always, it elevated those lives by affirming, even in the darkest of times, faith in the future.

Ratan is personally very optimistic and believes that when humankind is faced with its greatest challenges, it reaches its greatest levels of innovation. The challenges as well as triumphs of Tata in the time of Covid have certainly helped put the Cyrus Mistry dispute in perspective. Likely, the Mistry family will eventually exit Tata Sons, as their heavy investment in commercial real estate, of which the world has a massive oversupply, leaves them critically exposed.

~

Ratan was seventy-eight when he made the biggest decision of his business career. It was the decision to acknowledge that he had made a mistake when he had accepted the recommendation of the nomination committee to appoint Cyrus Mistry as the chairman of Tata Sons. Indeed, no less a body than the Supreme Court of India ratified the magnitude of that error. In dismissing, on 26 March 2021, the last-minute plea of the SP Group to evaluate its shares in Tata Sons 'for an honourable exit from Tata Sons through payment of fair compensation', Chief Justice S.A. Bobde wrote: 'In fact, it may be conceded today by Tata Sons that one important decision the board took on March 16, 2012 (appointment of Mistry as executive deputy chairman) certainly turned out to be the wrong decision of a lifetime.'[8]

Ratan had come to feel that, under Cyrus, Tata Sons was drifting away from the essence of the company founded by Jamsetji Tata, the crux summed up in Jamsetji's belief that 'what comes from the people must be returned to the people'. True, Tata Sons has publicly traded companies, but all the companies under the Tata Sons umbrella must contribute to Tata Sons dividends, if they make a profit. Tata Sons, in turn, must distribute 90 per cent of its net income to charitable causes. (It has the option of retaining 10 per cent for up to five years.)

In his three-page letter to Cyrus Mistry, which was written two years into Cyrus's tenure, Ratan made it very clear that he believed it was wrong for Tata Sons to be letting building contracts to companies controlled by the Mistry family. Ratan went so far as to say: 'This matter is so fundamental that if we cannot get it resolved between us, it will be necessary to have it become an issue of more public nature.'

Cyrus cannot claim that he was not warned. This letter was written on 24 September 2013. It was on 24 October three years later that Ratan finally ended the Mistry chairmanship.

Why did Ratan wait so long? There were several personal factors. Ratan's health had not been optimal. He suffered from severe foot pain and was having difficulty getting around. Also, I believe, he continued to hope that Cyrus would change and return to being the Cyrus Mistry whose appointment he had sanctioned. Instead, however, Mistry became increasingly distant and carried out several business transactions without board approval. I do not believe that any single transgression prompted Ratan to act, but many smaller actions demonstrated to him that Cyrus was not putting the interests of his largest shareholder, Tata Sons, first.

The important thing to remember is that when the Mistry family acquired their holdings in Tata Sons, it was a very tightly controlled, privately held company. They knew the day they bought in that there were very strict restrictions on selling their shares. Nothing has changed since then. That is why they were able to get them so cheaply. The fact that they have made hundreds of millions in dividends in no way changes the fact that they have very restricted ability to sell the shares or use them as collateral. Moreover, this was a restriction of which they were amply aware when they bought into the company.

The essence of the Supreme Court ruling was this: when you buy shares in a privately held company controlled by philanthropic trusts, you accept that you have very limited liquidity. You accept the terms and conditions of the Articles of Association of that company. You cannot later claim that you were unaware that, in essence, Tata Sons was, and is, a philanthropic organization. You cannot demand that the company be forced to change its Articles of Association.

The Mistry family argued that they were the victims in a case of suppression of minority rights. In fact, the case was precisely the opposite. The SP Group was a minority shareholder attempting to force its will on a majority shareholder.

Chief Justice Bobde observed the following with regard to refusing to involve the Supreme Court in determining the fair value of the SP Group shares: 'It is an irony that the very same person who represents shareholders owning just 18.37% of the total paid-up share capital and yet identified as the successor to the empire, has chosen to accuse the very same board of conduct oppressive and unfairly prejudicial to the interests of the minorities . . . the removal of a person from the post of executive chairman cannot be termed as oppressive or prejudicial.'[9]

I would speculate that some very long-term arrangement will be entered into, allowing the Mistry family to gradually sell down their shareholdings in the publicly traded Tata companies. Whatever understanding is reached, the process of selling will have to be done very gradually, to avoid adversely impacting the valuations of the public companies. So the final resolution of the rupture between the Mistrys and the Tatas will take considerable time.

But time is on the side of Tata Sons, which has been around for more than 150 years. Ratan Tata welcomed the Supreme Court's decision not as a personal victory but as 'a validation of the values and ethics that have always been the guiding principles of the group'.[10] Thus, Tata Sons will go on doing what no other company in the world does. *What comes from the people should go back to the people.* The spirit of Jamsetji may smile in contemplation of this most enduring, most unusual business he created.

Appendix A: Minutes of the Selection Committee

September 14, 2011

The Committee Meeting was held over lunch and the members briefly discussed the suitability of different candidates under two categories viz. (i) Internal and (ii) External. An attempt was made to rank those interviewed as 1 and 2 relating to the two categories and there were subsequent discussions on the subject, leading to a narrowing down of potential candidates.

The Committee thereafter interacted extensively with Mr. Cyrus Mistry (Mr. CM) since on the previous occasion the discussion was impromptu and needed more deliberations on both sides.

The gist of the interview is given below:-

- Q. What do you think about Tata?
- A. I have had the benefit of being on some Boards, but have not been involved in depth with the workings of the Companies. It is a business with a strong sense of social responsibility and a value system.
- Q. Why should I invest in Tata?
- A. Tata has not only a strong sense of social responsibility and values, but aims at value creation for all. To be too numbers oriented would be no better than being a portfolio manager. The financial side of the business, the business and technology cycles would all have to be evaluated and the effect on the Brand would have to be taken into account, if any divestment was considered.
- Q. Your articulation should be precise.
- A. One cannot take a view in a single dimension…the problems have to be viewed though multiple filters.
- Q. What in your view would be the way forward?
- A. Consolidation is essential, but one cannot stand still. I would look at growth but through conservative lens. A large number of seniors would be retiring soon and so creating a team both internally and externally would be essential and urgent. The re-constitution of the Boards of Companies would be essential, not merely the induction of individuals. Boards should be made robust. One must plan for growth, but not only look at return on capital but also at the long term creation of shareholder value.

- Q. You are the main individual shareholder in Tata Sons and therefore are you looking at yourself?
- A. I would look at the long term creation of value for all the stakeholders.
- Q. What horizon would you look at...2021? Which would be the core businesses of the Group? What would be your plans for TCS? Would any drastic change be needed in the Group? What would be
  your view on companies with a low return? Should they be   divested?
- A. This decision would have to be viewed through multiple filters....just low return would not be the only criteria to look at to make such a decision. For example it should be viewed as to whether or not the company was locked into a dying industry or a non -competitive industry. I would look at value addition, cash flow and to harvest the investment made.
- Q. Therefore would you exit the steel business?
- A. No. Other markets are still opening up.
- Q. Are you confusing value, vision and returns?
- A. All these are important as is the responsibility to the stake holders.
- Q. You run a company.....what is the plus from there that makes you competent to run Tata?
- A. I have contributed to growth and been challenged in various ways, which experience would be useful. I have no domain knowledge of certain businesses, but how you mange knowledge is very important.
- Q. Suppose you got this job, what would be the way forward?
- A. No change can happen overnight. The road map would have to be created. Relationships on the technical side would have to be created. There would have to be partnerships on all fronts to take matters forward.
- Q. Mr. RNT has got the instinct to acquire businesses and drop them when the do not work. Would you be able to do that?
- A. I would not at present be confident about doing this.
- Q. What was your contribution in Tata Power?
- A. Not enough.
- Q. Does Tata Sons operate as a Board or at one man's behest?
- A. It operates as a Board, but with the towering personality of the Chairman. If any views are expressed, the Chairman listens and then decisions are taken.
- Q. How would you run the Board?
- A. It needs a change as it is too inbred .
- Q. Therefore it is not really effective?
- A. Yes. Not as much as it should be.
- Q. How would you change it?
- A. I would have one third external directors who would bring a variety of inputs and have a strong understanding of business cycles and technology. The Board should also have a strong audit committee, a lawyer and Trust Nominees. This would strengthen governance of the Company.

- Q. How would you decide which would be the core businesses of the Group?
- A. Returns would not be the only touch stone. One would have to determine the key areas to assess the core businesses. This would be done by discussion with the team. Energies would not be diffused by going into too many areas. Opportunities must be seized, but opportunism shunned. TCS is very valuable, but most vulnerable.
- Q. Why was Corus bought? To get access to technology?
- A. To make the organization international; to globalize Tata and meet the need to grow.
- Q. One does not always take decisions only by analyzing the situation, but with vision and guts.
- A. Not to be scared of failure marks a leader.
- Q. But there may bold decisions to take and you may have to depend on others' domain knowledge.
- A. If I have the domain knowledge, I will go with it or trust others' knowledge in that field.
- Q. In some areas the Chairman does not have the required domain knowledge, and still is able to take management decisions there.
- A. I would build a team which will give these knowledge inputs. The CEO would have to be able to look deeper into matters and with the team be able to take risks. The challenge is to understand human capacity in an organization. But mistakes will be made.
- Q. What has been your interaction with Government?
- A. This has been a weakness as I have not had much interaction with Government as I depend on others for this. The Tata platform makes a good beginning.
- Q. What would be your stand on corruption? Mr. Tata's views are that there should be no compromise on this issue.
- A. I am equally uncomfortable with the corruption scene. I believe strengths have to be built here and that Tata should interact and engage with the bureaucracy. But who one should engage with should be carefully assessed.
- Q. What are your views on the direction Tata should take on the matter of being based here or abroad?
- A. There should be a substantial presence abroad, but not to go to the extent that Mr. Anshu Jain went in this matter.
- Q. You are an Irish citizen.....would you change that?
- A. Regardless of whether I got the job or not, I have been thinking of doing this for some time.
- Q. You own 18% of the shares of Tata Sons. How would you deflect the charge that you were doing things for yourself. How would you erect a Chinese wall?

- A. I have in the past even closed a business to my detriment so that I was not seen to be benefiting myself.

Appendix B: Articles of Association of the Tata Group

32

The Selection Committee shall comprise - (a) Three (3) persons nominated jointly by the Sir Dorabji Tata Trust and the Sir Ratan Tata Trust who may or may not be Directors of the Company, (b) one (1) person nominated by and from amongst the Board of Directors of the Company and (c) one (1) independent outside person selected by the Board for this purpose. The Chairman of the Committee will be selected by the Sir Dorabji Tata Trust and the Sir Ratan Tata Trust from amongst the nominees nominated by the Trusts.

The quorum for a meeting of the Selection Committee shall be the presence of a majority of members nominated jointly by the Sir Dorabji Tata Trust and the Sir Ratan Tata Trust.

** Explanation: The words 'nominated jointly' used in this Article shall mean that the Sir Dorabji Tata Trust and the Sir Ratan Tata Trust shall together decide the nominees. In the case of any difference, the decision of the majority of the Trustees in the aggregate of the Sir Dorabji Tata Trust and the Sir Ratan Tata Trust shall prevail.

119. APPOINTMENT OF DEPUTY CHAIRMAN / VICE CHAIRMAN

The Board of Directors of the Company may appoint from amongst the Directors of the Company, a Deputy Chairman and/or a Vice Chairman of the Board of Directors and shall have the right to remove such Deputy Chairman or Vice Chairman when deemed necessary.

120. ABSENCE OF CHAIRMAN AT BOARD MEETING

If at any meeting the Chairman of the Board shall not be present within fifteen minutes of the time appointed for holding the same, the Deputy Chairman and in his absence the Vice Chairman shall be the Chairman of the meeting and if the Deputy Chairman/Vice Chairman shall not be present, the Directors present shall choose one of their number to be the Chairman of such meeting.

121. MATTERS HOW DECIDED

Matters before any meeting of the Board which are required to be decided by a majority of the Directors shall require #the affirmative vote of a majority of the Directors appointed pursuant to Article 104B present at the meeting and in the case of an equality of votes the Chairman shall have a casting vote.

---

* Substituted vide Special Resolution passed at the Extraordinary General Meeting held on 6th December, 2012.

** Inserted vide Special Resolution passed at the Extraordinary General Meeting held on 9th April, 2014.

The words 'the affirmative vote of all the Directors appointed pursuant to Article 104B' has been substituted with the words 'the affirmative vote of a majority of the Directors appointed pursuant to Article 104B' vide Special Resolution passed at the Extraordinary General Meeting held on 9th April, 2014.

33

*121A.   The following matters shall be resolved upon by the Board of Directors:

(a)   A five year Strategic Plan that should include an assessment of the proposed strategic path of the Company, business and investment opportunities, proposed business and investment initiatives and a comparative analysis of similarly situated holding companies, and any alterations to such Strategic Plan;

(b)   An annual business plan structured to form part of the Strategic Plan, that should include proposed investments, incurring of debt, debt to equity ratio, debt service coverage ratio, projected cash flow of the Company and any alterations to such annual business plan;

(c)   The incurring or renewal of any debt or other borrowing by the Company, which debt or borrowing causes the cumulative outstanding debt of the Company, to exceed twice its net worth or which debt/borrowing is incurred/renewed at a time when the cumulative outstanding debt of the Company has already exceeded twice its net worth, if not already approved as part of the annual business plan;

(d)   Any proposed investment by the Company in securities, shares, stocks, bonds, debentures, financial instruments of any sort or immovable property, of a value exceeding Rs. 100 crores if not already approved as part of the annual business plan;

(e)   Any increase in the authorized, subscribed, issued or paid up capital of the Company and any issue or allotment of shares by the Company (whether on a rights basis or otherwise);

(f)   Any sale or pledge, mortgage or other encumbrance or creation of any right or interest by the Company of or over its shareholding in any Tata company or of or over any part thereof, if not already approved as part of the annual business plan;

(g)   Any matter affecting the shareholding of the Tata Trusts in the Company or the rights conferred upon the Tata Trusts by the Articles of the Company or the shareholding of the Company in any Tata Company if not already approved as part of the annual business plan;

(h)   Exercise of the voting rights of the Company at the general meetings of any Tata Company, including the appointment of a representative of the Company under Section 113(1)(a) of the Companies Act, 2013 in respect of a general meeting of any Tata Company and, in any manner concerning the raising of capital, incurring of debt and divesting or acquisition of any undertaking or business of such Tata Company, instructions to such representative on how to exercise the Company's voting rights.

Explanation: The term "Tata Company" used in this Article shall, as the context requires, mean each or any of the following companies:

Tata Consultancy Services Limited, Tata Steel Limited, Tata Motors Limited, Tata Capital Limited, Tata Chemicals Ltd., The Tata Power Company Limited, Tata Global Beverages Limited, The Indian Hotels Company Limited, Trent   Limited, Tata Teleservices (Maharashtra) Limited, Tata Industries Limited, Tata Teleservices Limited, Tata Communications Limited, Titan Company Limited and Infiniti Retail Limited and any other company in which the Company (or its subsidiaries) holds twenty percent or more of the paid up share capital and whose name is notified in writing to the Company by the Directors nominated under Article 104B."

---

* Inserted vide Special Resolution passed at the Extraordinary General Meeting held on 9th April, 2014.

Appendix C: Letter from Ratan Tata to Cyrus Mistry, Dated 24 September 2013

PERSONAL & STRICTLY CONFIDENTIAL

ELPHINSTONE BUILDING • 3RD FLOOR • 10 VEER NARIMAN ROAD • MUMBAI 400 001 • PHONE (022) 6665 8000

September 24, 2013

Dear Cyrus,

As I mentioned at our last meeting, the position you have taken on transactions between Tata Group companies and your family businesses in which you have a significant personal beneficial interest has resulted in a major fundamental conflict between us. Your position demolishes in spirit and reality the values and ethical standards set by Jamsetji Tata, assiduously followed by successive chairmen in order to safeguard and perpetuate the founder's ideals which have differentiated us from others.

When your candidature was suggested for the position of Tata Sons Chairman, I wholeheartedly supported the proposal, but told the committee that the most crucial issue would be how you disassociated yourself from your family businesses so as to ensure that there was no conflict of interest brought about by your personal holdings in Tata group companies or in the project/contracting areas. The committee confirmed that this had been discussed with you and that you had agreed that this would be resolved in a legal manner to the satisfaction of the group.

You and I have discussed this matter on more than one occasion, and I left it to you to act on this in an appropriate manner, but as nothing meaningful has been settled I raised it with you again the other day. We had earlier discussed the creation of a blind trust as a means of disassociating yourself from your Tata shareholding. You had said that this was not possible in India, but I now understand that such a legal instrument is indeed possible here.

ELPHIN STONE BUILDING • 3RD FLOOR • 10 VEER NARIMAN ROAD • MUMBAI 400 001 • PHONE (022) 6665 8000

2

Similarly, the cleanest way to avoid conflict of interest on the project/contracting side is not to engage in any transaction of business between your family contracting/project companies and the Tata Group so long as you are Chairman. This is a widely practised policy globally. It is also enshrined in our Code of Conduct document, prepared 15 years ago. Everyone would expect the Group Chairman to lead by example, and to set the tone and ethical standards for all employees. Your view that this can be controlled by monitoring tender conditions and contract management will not be effective. Preparation of tilted tender documents, the clandestine sharing of information, escalation claims and changes in the scope of work are amongst the areas open to abuse. In this case, which employee, committee or external agency is going to be totally neutral or just in a contract where the Group Chairman has a personal beneficial interest of 50%? What would be the public perception of situations where contracts are awarded to your family business for building a plant, housing colony or hotel or major infrastructure where you personally have a 50% ownership interest? Will these be practices which will stand the test of public scrutiny? I think not! How will you as Chairman take responsibility for upholding the values of the house amongst all employees if you cannot lead by example? What happens on projects where your companies and Tatas bid on projects competitively in India and overseas, or where disputes arise? Will all these stand the test of public scrutiny also?

Over the past year, I have made every effort to be supportive of all your actions and decisions, providing my views only if sought, I have ensured that I do not become "a ghost in the corridor".

ELPHIN STONE BUILDING • 3RD FLOOR • 10 VEER NARIMAN ROAD • MUMBAI 400 001 • PHONE (022) 6665 8000

3

You must however recognise and understand that I will make every effort to safeguard what I believe is in the interest of the Trusts, where I remain responsible, to ensure that the values and ethical standards which have been one of our main foundations and our major differentiator are in no way eroded or compromised.

This matter is so fundamental that if it cannot be resolved between us it will necessarily have to become an issue of a more public nature.

I hope this rather long letter conveys the context and the concerns that have caused this conflict to arise.

With regards,

Ratan

Appendix D: Letter from Ratan Tata to Cyrus Mistry, Dated 22 August 2014

TATA TRUSTS

AUGUST 22, 2014

RATAN N. TATA
CHAIRMAN

Dear Cyrus,

YOU WILL RECALL I HAD WRITTEN TO YOU ON JULY 1ST SUGGESTING THAT FOR THE SAKE OF FULL TRANSPARENCY AND GOVERNANCE IT WOULD BE APPROPRIATE FOR A TABULATION OF CONTRACTS ENTERED INTO WITH SHAPOORJI PALLONJI/STERLING MOTORS WHICH EXISTED BEFORE YOUR OFFICE ORDER TO VARIOUS COMPANIES IN OCTOBER BE PREPARED AND PUT BEFORE THE BOARDS OF EACH CONCERNED COMPANY, TATA SONS AND THE TATA TRUSTS GIVING THE DATES OF CONTRACT FULFILMENT.

YOU RESPONDED PROMPTLY TO MY LETTER INDICATING THAT YOU WERE PASSING INSTRUCTIONS FOR THIS TO BE DONE. I KNOW THAT YOU HAVE MANY THINGS ON YOUR MIND AND ON YOUR SCHEDULE BUT I JUST THOUGHT I WOULD SEND YOU THIS REMINDER AS THIS MATTER REMAINS AN OPEN ISSUE AND I BELIEVE THIS SHOULD BE SETTLED.

WOULD YOU PLEASE INDICATE WHEN SUCH A TABULATION WOULD BE AVAILABLE? SUCH A TABULATION OF EXISTING DATA SHOULD NOT NORMALLY TAKE MORE THAN A FEW DAYS AS IT MERELY COMPILES EXISTING DATA IN THE PUBLIC DOMAIN. I AM THEREFORE BRINGING THIS TO YOUR ATTENTION AS I BELIEVE THIS IS A NECESSARY ACTION TO DEAL WITH THIS LONGSTANDING MATTER.

WITH REGARDS,

YOURS SINCERELY,

RATAN N. TATA

MR. CYRUS MISTRY
CHAIRMAN
TATA SONS
MUMBAI

SIR DORABJI TATA TRUST · SIR RATAN TATA TRUST · JAMSETJI TATA TRUST · THE N. R. TATA TRUST · J. R. D. TATA TRUST

ELPHINSTONE BUILDING, 3RD FLOOR, 10 VEER NARIMAN ROAD, MUMBAI 400 001, INDIA
TEL. 91 22 6665 8000 FAX 91 22 6665 8001 EMAIL RNT@TATA.COM

Appendix E: A History of Shareholding by S.P. Mistry Group Entities (1964 to December 2016)

Tata Sons Limited
History of shareholding by S P Mistry group entities - 1964 to December 2016 - Summary

Date	Particulars	T Sons' Equity Share Capital		Shareholding by Tata Trusts		Shareholding by T Cos, Individuals, Others		Shareholding by Shapoorji Pallonji Mistry entities			
		FV/Sh (A)	Shares (B)	Shares (C)	% of Eq. Capital (D)	Shares (E)	% of Eq. Capital (F)	Shares (G)	% of Eq. Capital (H)	Cost/Sh [Rs] (I)	Cost [Rs Crore] (J)
01-Jan-65	Shareholding Pattern before purchases by SP Group	4,500	2,079	1,724	82.92%	355	17.08%	-	0.00%	-	-
15-Jan-65	Purchase by SP Group from R Sawhney					(124)	-5.96%	124	5.96%	9,153	0.11
	Shareholding Pattern after purchase	4,500	2,079	1,724	82.92%	231	11.11%	124	5.96%		
Jul-69	Purchase by SP Group from Ratan Tata Trust			(900)	-4.81%			900	4.81%	1,490	0.11
	Shareholding Pattern after purchase	1,000	18,711	14,481	77.39%	2,214	11.83%	2,016	10.77%		
29-May-74	Purchase by SP Group from D R D Tata					(1,875)	-6.68%	1,875	6.68%	1,050	0.13
	Shareholding Pattern after purchase	1,000	28,066	21,798	77.67%	1,369	4.88%	4,899	17.46%		
	Shareholding Pattern before Rights Issue in 1995	1,000	1,49,684	1,17,272	78.35%	6,288	4.20%	26,124	17.45%		
11-Sep-95	Rights Issue Sep 1995 : 1 sh for 5 sh held, at Rs 100,000 / Sh	1,000	29,937			23,016		6,921		1,00,000	69.21
29-Dec-16	Shareholding Pattern after Rights Issue & on date	1,000	4,04,146	2,63,852	66.29%	65,933	16.31%	74,352	18.40%		69.57
	Value of T Sons holding at March 2016 (Rs Crore)		3,17,658	2,07,395		51,823					58,441

Notes :

1. Holding of MK Tata Trust is grouped with 'T Cos, Individuals, Others'. MK Tata Trust held 15 shares of FV Rs 4,500 per share at December 1964 and 2,421 shares of FV Rs 1,000 per share at 23 December 2016.

2. Cost of purchases by S P group entities mentioned in Columns I & J are as per the Transfer Deeds.

Source: R. Venkataramanan, former chair of the Tata Trusts

Appendix F: The Tata Family Tree

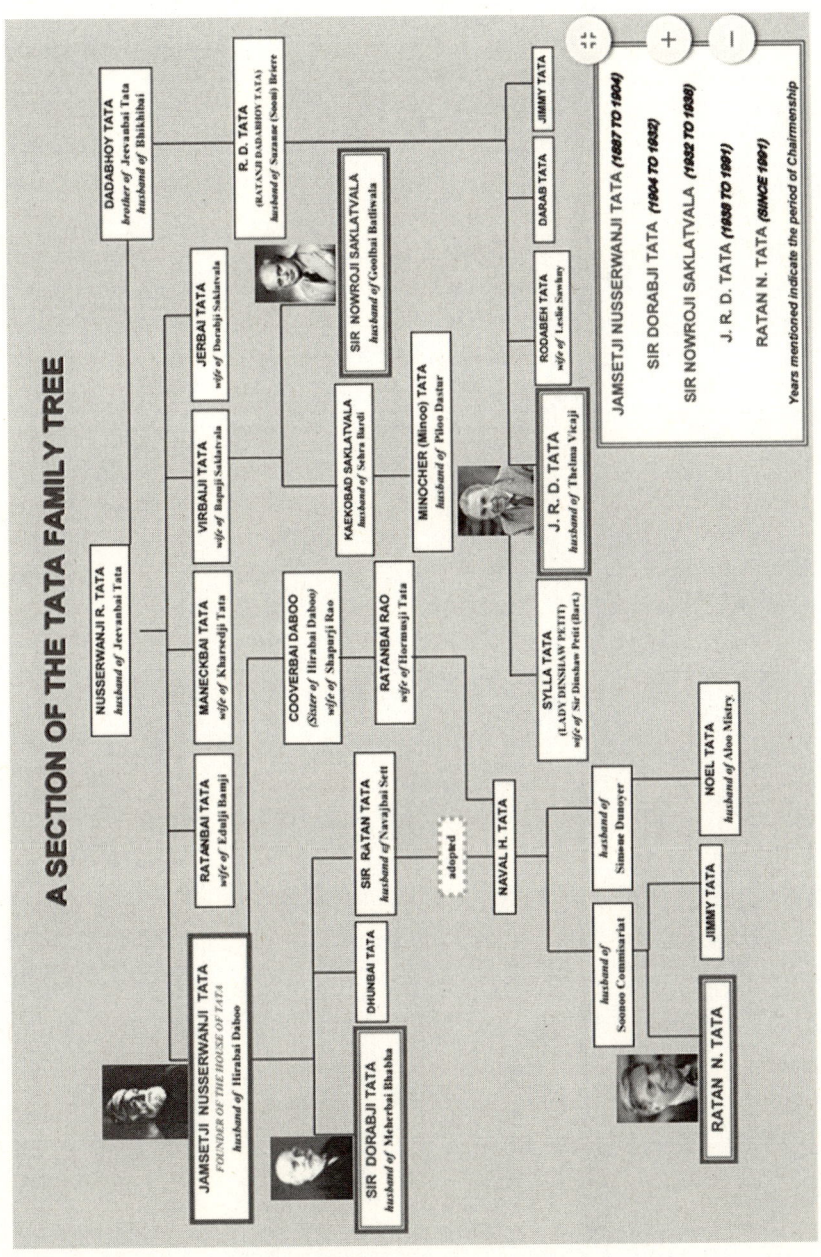

A SECTION OF THE TATA FAMILY TREE

JAMSETJI NUSSERWANJI TATA
FOUNDER OF THE HOUSE OF TATA
husband of Hirabai Daboo

DADABHOY TATA
brother of Jeevanbai Tata
husband of Bhikhibai

R. D. TATA
(RATANJI DADABHOY TATA)
husband of Suzanne (Sooni) Briere

NUSSERWANJI R. TATA
husband of Jeevanbai Tata

RATANBAI TATA
wife of Edulji Bamji

MANECKBAI TATA
wife of Kharsedji Tata

VIRBAIJI TATA
wife of Bapuji Saklatvala

JERBAI TATA
wife of Dorabji Saklatvala

SIR NOWROJI SAKLATVALA
husband of Goolbai Batliwala

KAEKOBAD SAKLATVALA
husband of Sehra Bardi

MINOCHER (Minoo) TATA
husband of Piloo Dastur

COOVERBAI DABOO
(Sister of Hirabai Daboo)
wife of Shapurji Rao

RATANBAI RAO
wife of Hormusji Tata

J. R. D. TATA
husband of Thelma Vicaji

JIMMY TATA

DARAB TATA

RODABEH TATA
wife of Leslie Sawhay

SYLLA TATA
(LADY DINSHAW PETIT)
wife of Sir Dinshaw Petit (Bart.)

DHUNBAI TATA

SIR DORABJI TATA
husband of Meherbai Bhabha

SIR RATAN TATA
husband of Navajbai Sett

adopted

NAVAL H. TATA

husband of
Soonoo Commisariat

husband of
Simone Dunoyer

NOEL TATA
husband of Aloo Mistry

JIMMY TATA

RATAN N. TATA

JAMSETJI NUSSERWANJI TATA (1887 TO 1904)

SIR DORABJI TATA (1904 TO 1932)

SIR NOWROJI SAKLATVALA (1932 TO 1938)

J. R. D. TATA (1938 TO 1991)

RATAN N. TATA (SINCE 1991)

Years mentioned indicate the period of Chairmenship

Source: Tata Central Archives

Notes

Prologue

1. Ann Graham, 'Too Good to Fail', *Strategy+Business* 58 (Spring 2010), 23 February 2010, https://bit.ly/2mUQIaA.
2. Ratan Tata, in an interview with the author, 2 November 2016.
3. Tata group financials, Tata.com, https://bit.ly/2NXox6d.
4. 'The quotable Jamsetji Tata', Tata.com, March 2008, http://bit.ly/2XLrs8a.
5. Andrew Carnegie, 'The Gospel of Wealth', in *The Gospel of Wealth and Other Timely Essays* (New York: Century Company, 1901), pp. 1–46.

Chapter 1: 'Go on Doing My Work and Increasing It'

1. Srividhya Iyer, 'Cyrus Mistry fired! Here's all you need to know about who he is and why TATA said Tata to its Group Chairman', India.com, 24 October 2016, https://bit.ly/2K7jy0g.
2. Sanjay Banerji, 'The Noise around Cyrus Mistry's Firing', NDTV.com, 1 November 2016, https://bit.ly/2NW0WTv.
3. Jai Madan, 'Where it all Began', in *The Legend and His Legacy: A Tribute to Tata Founder Jamsetji Tata*, Tata.com (a Tata Review Publication), 3 March 2014.
4. Good Thoughts, Good Words and Good Deeds: these maxims control the daily lives of the Zoroastrians. This drives the community to take concrete action to enhance the lives of the people in the local community, society and nation in general. In India, the Zoroastrians, who are also known as the Parsis, played a pivotal role in nation-building. The Tata family, the Godrej family and Mr Cyrus Poonawalla, to name a few from the community, played significant roles in developing India.
5. R.M. Lala, *For the Love of India: The Life and Times of Jamsetji Tata* (New Delhi: Penguin Books India, 2004), p. 16.

6.   Yagya Sharma, *Jamsetji Tata: The Man Who Saw Tomorrow* (Mumbai: Amar Chitra Katha, 2006), p. 2.

7.   Lala, *For the Love of India*, pp. 12–19.

8.   Ibid., p. 16.

9.   F.R. Harris, *Jamsetji Nusserwanji Tata: A Chronicle of His Life* (Bombay: Blackie & Son, 1958), p. 5.

10. Ibid., p. 4.

11. Id., pp. 5–6.

12. Id., p. 6.

13. Id., pp. 6–7.

14. Id., pp. 7–9.

15. Madan, 'Where it all Began', p. 5.

16. I have found two books especially helpful in understanding and appreciating Zoroastrianism: Mark Shah, *Zoroastrianism: An Introduction to Zoroastrianism* (N.p.: Amazon Digital Services, 2016); and Jenny Rose, *Zoroastrianism: An Introduction* (London: I.B. Tauris, 2011).

17. Harris, *Jamsetji Nusserwanji Tata*, pp. 13–14.

18. Ibid., p. 24.

19. Peter Casey, *The World's Greatest Company* (Bray, Republic of Ireland: Ballpoint Press, 2013), pp. 10–21; Tata, 'The giant who touched tomorrow', Tata.com, April 2004, http://bit.ly/2OJNLaf.

20. When Vaidya died in 1900, the Taj was completed by the same British civil engineer who had built the Watson, W.A. Chambers.

21. Cathy Scott-Clark and Adrian Levy, *The Siege: 68 Hours Inside the Taj Hotel* (New York: Penguin Books, 2013), p. 7.

22. Ratan Tata, in an interview with the author, July 2016.

23. Statistics from 'Taj Mahal Palace Hotel', Wikipedia.com, https://bit.ly/2vhrNm7.

24. 'The quotable Jamsetji Tata', Tata.com, March 2008, *http://bit.ly/2XLrs8a*.

25. 'About Sir Dorabji Tata', TataTrusts.org, https://bit.ly/2v3v742.

26. Ratanji was married to Lady Navajbai (1877–1965), the younger daughter of Ardeshir Merwanji Sett.

27. 'More Than a Businessman', Tata.com, https://www.tata.com/about-us/tata-group-our-heritage/tata-titans/sir-ratan-tata.

28. Ibid.

29. Id.

30. Boria Majumdar and Nalin Mehta, *India and the Olympics* (New York: Routledge, 2009), p. 9.

31. 'Tata's Olympic safari', *Times of India*, 3 August 2008, http://bit.ly/33hVOjF.

32. Majumdar and Mehta, *India and the Olympics*, p. 10.

33. Ibid.

34. Id.

35. 'In the name of the father', Tata.com, https://www.tata.com/about-us/tata-group-our-heritage/tata-titans/sir-dorabji-tata.

36. 'Dorabji Tata while laying the foundation stone of the Lonavala Dam, 8th February 1911', Tatasteel.com.

37. R.M. Lala, *Beyond the Last Blue Mountain: A Life of J.R.D. Tata* (Gurgaon: Penguin Random House India, 2017)

38. Jehangir Pocha, 'Tata Sons: Passing the Baton', *Forbes India*, 12 December 2011, http://bit.ly/2QO5eRz.

39. Ratan Tata, in an interview with the author, July 2016.

40. The man who played from the heart', Tata.com, https://www.tata.com/about-us/tata-group-our-heritage/tata-titans/sir-nowroji-saklatvala.

Chapter 2: Ratan Tata: The First Years

1. Ratan Tata, in an interview with the author, July 2016.

2. Ibid.

3. Id.

4. Morgen Witzel, *Tata: The Evolution of a Corporate Brand* (New Delhi: Penguin Books India, 2010), p. 180.

5. 'A life lived from the heart', Tata.com, April 2004, https://www.tata.com/about-us/tata-group-our-heritage/tata-titans/naval-tata.

6. Noel Tata, in an interview with the author, Trent offices, Mumbai, 4 August 2017.

7. Randeep Ramesh, 'The Tatas are a reconstructed family. They promote talent rather than blood relations. Ratan was clearly talented', *Guardian*, 27 March 2008, http://bit.ly/35yOIJi.

8. Gita Piramal, *Business Maharajas* (New Delhi: Penguin Books India, 2000), p. 371.

9. Soumyadipta Banerjee, 'Life was quite a drudgery in my childhood: Ratan Tata', *DNA*, 20 July 2010, http://bit.ly/2DkOUQ4.

10. Ibid.

11. Id.

12. See 'Notable alumni' in 'Cathedral and John Connon School', Wikipedia.com, http://bit.ly/33kEn27.

13. Banerjee, 'Life was quite a drudgery in my childhood: Ratan Tata'.

14. Mehernaaz Shovir Irani, 'Ratan Tata Addresses Cathedral and John Connon School Alumni', *Parsi Khabar*, 31 March 2009, http://bit.ly/2DeFmWY.

15. arZan, 'Ratan Tata, India's humble business king', *Parsi Khabar*, 19 May 2009, http://bit.ly/2KRjDIH.

16. Irani, 'Ratan Tata Addresses Cathedral and John Connon School Alumni'.

17. Ramesh, 'The Tatas are a reconstructed family. They promote talent rather than blood relations. Ratan was clearly talented'.

18. Ibid.

19. K.E. Eduljee, 'Zoroastrian Demographics: Population Statistics, Diaspora and Group Names', HeritageInstitute.com, https://bit.ly/2OCjUQ4.

20. Laurie Goldstein, 'Zoroastrians Keep the Faith, and Keep Dwindling', *New York Times*, 6 September 2006, https://nyti.ms/2vtzCo4.

21. See Mark Shah, *Zoroastrianism: An Introduction to Zoroastrianism* (N.p.: Amazon Digital Services, 2016); and Jenny Rose, *Zoroastrianism: An Introduction* (London: I.B. Tauris, 2011).

Chapter 3: From the Factory Floor

1. Ratan Tata, in an interview with the author, November 2016.

2. Noel Tata, in an interview with the author, Trent offices, Mumbai, 4 August 2017.

3. Ratan Tata, in an interview with the author, July 2016.

4. 'Ratan Tata '59: The Cornell Story', College of Architecture, Art and Planning (AAP), CornellCast, Cornell University, 2 August 2011, https://bit.ly/2vFg7Zx.

5. Ibid.

6. Ratan Tata, in an interview with the author, July 2016.

7. Ibid.

8. The Tata-Cornell Institute for Agriculture and Nutrition (TCI), Cornell University, https://bit.ly/2LXLqdq.

9. Ratan Tata, in an interview with the author, July 2016.

10. 'Ratan Tata '59: The Cornell Story', College of Architecture, Art and Planning (AAP), CornellCast, Cornell University.

11. Gita Piramal, *Business Maharajas* (New Delhi: Penguin Books India, 1997), p. 329, https://bit.ly/2MgTKRl.

12. Ibid., p. 329.

13. Id., p. 329.

14. Id., pp. 329–30.

15. Id., p. 330.
16. Harvard 'Advanced Management Program: Transforming Proven Leaders into Global Executives', Harvard Business School, Soldiers Field, Boston, Massachusetts, https://hbs.me/2AJaj7g.
17. 'Felt Confused and humiliated during early Harvard days: Ratan Tata', *Times of India* 12 December 2013, https://hbs.me/2AJaj7g.
18. Ibid.
19. Id.
20. 'Ratan Tata and NELCO Crucible—the untold story', *Vivify* (blog), 11 October 2013, https://bit.ly/2LQxyBo.; and Piramal, *Business Maharajas*, p. 330.
21. Piramal, *Business Maharajas*, p. 331.
22. Ibid., p. 331.
23. Id. (italics added).
24. Id.
25. Id., pp. 331–32.
26. Id., p. 333.
27. Id., p. 334; and Shiv Taneja, 'Hotting up: Workers intensify agitation', *India Today*, 15 November 1989, https://bit.ly/2vmQ5Lm.
28. Piramal, *Business Maharajas*, p. 335.
29. Taneja, 'Hotting up: Workers intensify agitation'.
30. Piramal, *Business Maharajas*, p. 336.
31. Ibid.
32. Id.
33. 'TATA group history (Timeline created by Abhijit)', Timetoast.com, http://bit.ly/34hBjoG.

Chapter 4: Mission and Values

1. Damian Whitworth, 'The Empire Strikes Back: The Tata Legacy', *The Times*, 27 May 2006, reprinted in 'The Empire strikes back', Tata.com, https://www.thetimes.co.uk/article/ratan-tata-the-mumbai-tycoon-collecting-british-brands-7svmghsjkbg.
2. Ibid.
3. Id.
4. Id.
5. Id.
6. Id.
7. Id.

8.   Id.

9.   Ratan Tata, 'A world to win', Tata.com, June 2005.

10. Ratan Tata, in an interview with the author, July 2016.

11. Ratan Tata, in an interview with the author, November 2016.

12. C. Narayana Rao Chennai, 'Five Guiding Principles of JRD Tata', *Inspirational Musings* (blog), 10 March 2008, https://bit.ly/2nesyrB.

13. Ratan Tata, in an interview with the author, November 2017.

14. 'Nano Wars', *The Economist*, 28 April 2008, https://econ.st/2Mkmitb.

15. Vir Sanghvi, 'Ratan Tata', VirSanghvi.com, 24 July 2005, https://bit.ly/2OhvGyC.

16. Ibid.

17. Christabelle Noronha, 'Vision of the Future', Tata.com, August 2006.

18. For a useful overview of the controversy, see 'Singur Tata Nano controversy', Wikipedia.com, https://bit.ly/2NjGTy1.

19. Gita Piramal, *Business Maharajas* (New Delhi: Penguin Books India, 1997), p. 334; Shiv Taneja, 'Hotting up: Workers intensify agitation', *India Today*, 15 November 1989, https://bit.ly/2vmQ5Lm.

20. 'Ratan Tata's words of inspiration', Rediff.com, 26 August 2008, https://bit.ly/2vmsmef. Also see Kevin and Jackie Freiberg, *Nanovation: How a Little Car Can Teach the World to Think Big* (Nashville: Thomas Nelson, 2011), p. 119.

21. Ratan Tata, telephone interview with the author, November 2017.

22. 'Ms Banerjee Pulled The Trigger', *Outlook*, 3 October 2008, http://bit.ly/2XJN84G.

23. Christabelle Noronha, 'Vision of the Future'.

24. Sumantra B. Barooah, 'Tata Motors' air-powered car project still on, to be launch ready in 3 years', *Autocar Professional*, 14 February 2017, https://bit.ly/2lf7em4.

25. Ratan Tata, in a telephone interview with the author, November 2017.

26. 'SCOOP! Tata Electric Nano will be launched as the Jayem Neo', *Autocar India*, 24 November 2017, https://bit.ly/2KB8cSy.

27. Ratan Tata, in an interview with the author, July 2016.

28. Christabelle Noronha, 'Treating the customer as king', Tata.com, March 2003.

29. Ibid.

30. Id.

31. Id.

32. Id.

33. Noronha, 'Vision of the Future'.

34. Ibid.

35. Id.

36. Id.

37. Id.

38. Id.

39. Id.

40. Id.

Chapter 5: Challenges

1. Gita Piramal, *Business Maharajas* (New Delhi: Penguin Books India, 1996), Chapter 7.

2. Gita Piramal, 'The Reluctant Tycoon', *Economic Times*, 10 November 1996.

3. Ratan Tata, interview with the author, July 2016.

4. Piramal, 'The Reluctant Tycoon'.

5. Dharminder Kumar, 'How history will come full circle if Tatas buy Air India', *Economic Times*, 21 June 2017, http://bit.ly/2rnltdM.

6. Piramal, 'The Reluctant Tycoon'.

7. Kumar, 'How history will come full circle if Tatas buy Air India'.

8. Piramal, *Business Maharajas*, Chapter 7.

9. Piramal, 'The Reluctant Tycoon'.

10. 'US jury slaps $940 million fine on Tata group in trade secret case', *Times of India*, 16 April 2016, http://bit.ly/2XJOOLw; and Regina Vogel Culbert, 'Epic Verdict in Trade Secrets Case', Lexology.com, 21 April 2016, https://bit.ly/2Ksnlpn.

11. Akanksha Jayanthi, 'Epic asks court to reduce $940M awarded in Tata case', BeckersHospitalReview.com, 15 June 2016, https://bit.ly/2LYNqlx.

12. Ratan Tata, interview with the author, July 2016.

13. Ibid.

14. Quoted in Piramal, *Business Maharajas*, Chapter 7.

15. Ibid.

16. Randeep Ramesh, 'The Tatas are a reconstructed family. They promote talent rather than blood relations. Ratan was clearly talented', *Guardian*, 27 March 2008, http://bit.ly/35yOIJi.

17. 'I have always tried to do the "right thing", says Ratan Tata," *DNA*, 7 December 2012, http://bit.ly/2ru8qHy.

18. Ibid.

19. Id.

20. Morgen Witzel, *Tata: The Evolution of a Corporate Brand* (New Delhi: Penguin Books India, 2011), p. 144.

21. Piramal, *Business Maharajas*, Chapter 7.

22. Ratan Tata, interview with the author, July 2016.

23. 'Annual Report 2009–10', Tata Consultancy Services, TCS.com, https://on.tcs.com/2AIG5Bt.

24. 'Investor Relations', Tata Consultancy Services, TCS.com, https://on.tcs.com/2M2ldJI.

25. 'Tata to Corus', Editorial, *The Hindu*, 1 April 2016, https://bit.ly/2MligRf.

26. Christabelle Noronha, 'Treating the Customer as King', Tata.com, March 2003, http://www.tata.com/aboutus/articlesinside/lY!$$$$!v0UIcUDM=/TLYVr3YPkMU.

27. 'Markets are taking a short-term', Rediff.com, 1 February 2007, https://www.rediff.com/money/2007/feb/01corus5.htm.

28. Rajesh Pandathil and Kishor Kadam, 'Tata Steel's failure with Corus and Tata Motors' success with JLR: A tale of 2 buyouts in 9 charts', Firstpost, 1 April 2016, http://bit.ly/37DYBHk.

29. See Christopher Gergen and Gregg Vanourek, *Life Entrepreneurs: Ordinary People Creating Extraordinary Lives* (San Francisco: Jossey-Bass, 2008), p. 97.

30. Rita McGrath, 'Failure Is a Gold Mine for India's Tata', *Harvard Business Review*, 11 April 2011, https://hbr.org/2011/04/failure-is-a-gold-mine-for-ind.

31. 'Celebrating innovation', Tata.com, April 2012.

32. Pandathil and Kadam, 'Tata Steel's failure with Corus and Tata Motors' success with JLR: A tale of 2 buyouts in 9 charts'.

33. Vikas Bajaj, 'Tata Motors Finds Success in Jaguar Land Rover', *New York Times*, 30 August 2012, https://nyti.ms/33jS3KS.

Chapter 6: How to Handle Even the Worst of Times

1. Marie Brenner, 'Anatomy of a Siege', *Vanity Fair*, 30 September 2009, https://bit.ly/2OloBNb.

2. Ron Moreau, 'India-Pakistan Tensions Grow in Wake of Attacks', *Newsweek*, 26 November 2008, https://bit.ly/2ORyByZ.

3. Clark Cathy Scott-Clark and Adrian Levy, *The Siege: 68 Hours Inside the Taj Hotel* (New York: Penguin Books, 2013), pp. 62–63.

4. 'Timeline of the 2008 Mumbai attacks', Wikipedia.com (sourced from NDTV, the *Evening Standard* and the BBC), https://bit.ly/2vPYNRE.

5.   Throughout 27–29 November 2008, the Oberoi Trident Hotel and Nariman House, a Chabad-Lubavitch Jewish Center in the Colaba neighbourhood, were also under attack, with loss of life and injury. The impression is of an entire city under attack.

6.   Clark and Levy, *The Siege*, p. 295.

7.   Letter sent by Duke of Wellington to John Croker, 8 August 1815, in *The History of England from the Accession of James II* (1848) by Thomas Babington Macaulay, Vol. I, Chapter 5.

8.   Taylor Gandossy, 'Taj Mahal hotel chairman: We had warning', CNN.com, 29 November 2008, https://cnn.it/2OTpxty.

9.   Clark and Levy, *The Siege*, p. 27.

10. Gandossy, 'Taj Mahal hotel chairman: We had warning'.

11. Clark and Levy, *The Siege*, p. 85.

12. Brenner, 'Anatomy of a Siege'.

13. Gandossy, 'Taj Mahal hotel chairman: We had warning'.

14. Raymond Bickson, 'Our Hotel Was Attacked', *New York Times*, 7 February 2008, https://nyti.ms/2vKUozC.

15. Rohit Deshpande and Anjali Raina, 'The Ordinary Heroes of the Taj', *Harvard Business Review*, December 2011, https://bit.ly/1WWsJRP.

16. Ibid.

17. Id.

18. Id.

19. Id.

20. Id.

21. Clark and Levy, *The Siege*, p. 72.

22. Ibid., p. 77.

23. Id., pp. 78–79.

24. Id., p. 79.

25. Reeba Zachariah and Vispashana V.K., 'As star chef Hemant Oberoi hangs up his apron, Taj set for a new taste', *Times of India*, 27 March 2015, https://bit.ly/2OkCmvw.

26. 'Valiant Kitchen Brigade took terrorists' bullets for guests', *Times of India*, 31 October 2013, https://bit.ly/2KEntSJ.

27. 'Mumbai Taj hostages freed, Ratan Tata slams attacks', LiveMint, 27 November 2008, https://bit.ly/2vpKnZs.

28. '26/11 attack a life-changing moment for me: Ratan Tata', *Times of India*, 2 December 2015, https://bit.ly/2OUc7NA.

29. Bickson, 'Our Hotel Was Attacked'.

30. A. Ganesh Nadar, '13/7 blasts: "Others have God, we have the Tatas"', Rediff.com, 13 July 2012, https://bit.ly/2B34kKT.

31. 'Ratan Tata dedicates restored Taj Hotel to terror victims', Rediff.com, 21 December 2008, https://bit.ly/2Md7vUk.

32. Bickson, 'Our Hotel Was Attacked'.

33. Ibid.

34. Quoted in Prateekshja M. Tiwari, *Pride of the Nation: Ratan Tata* (New Delhi: Diamond Books, 2015), p. 195.

35. Rina Chandran, 'Mumbai's Taj hotel reopens Sunday after 2008 attacks', *Business Travel*, 15 October 2010, https://reut.rs/2vS3PgS.

36. Richard Orange, 'Restoring the Taj is just part of Tata's challenge', *Spectator*, 7 January 2009, https://bit.ly/2vvjnHI.

37. Ibid.

38. Id.

Chapter 7: Relationships

1. Jehangir Pocha, 'Tata Sons: Passing the Baton', *Forbes India*, 12 December 2011, https://bit.ly/2eV1AjJ.

2. Sajeet Manghat, 'The Mistry Family Came on Board Tata Sons by Chance and May Exit by Force', Bloomberg/Quint, 7 November 2016, https://bit.ly/2vS6asa.

3. 'View: Why Ratan Tata was right about Cyrus Mistry and Tata Sons', *Economic Times*, 18 December 2016, https://bit.ly/2MtJ9mp.

4. Jayshree P. Upadhyay, 'Sebi finds no violation of norms at Tata companies', LiveMint, 4 August 2017, https://bit.ly/2M5Nsbd.

Chapter 8: The Future

1. Ratan Tata, in an interview with the author, 2 November 2016.

2. Tata Trusts, 'Chairman, Mr. Ratan N Tata's statement on Tata Trusts' COVID-19 strategy', press release, 28 March 2020, https://bit.ly/2RlcXZL.

3. P.B. Jayakumar, 'Coronavirus: Tata Trusts building four COVID-19 treatment hospitals', *Business Today*, 16 May 2020, https://bit.ly/3ude7Fe.

4. Natarajan Chandrasekaran, 'Tata Group's Response to Covid-19', Tata. com, July 2020, https://bit.ly/3eNnCV8.

5. Ibid.

6. Dev Chatterjee, 'Covid-19 crisis: Ratan Tata says layoffs show India Inc's lack of empathy', *Business Standard*, 24 July 2020, https://bit.ly/33gpYGp.

7. Rajeev Singhal, Subodh Pandey, et al., 'Applying the Lessons of the Pandemic to Build for the Future', BCG.com, 20 October 2020, https://on.bcg.com/3tfigXE.

8. Judgement of the Hon'ble Supreme Court of India dated 26 Match 2021 in *Tata Consultancy Services Ltd Versus Cyrus Investments Pvt Ltd and Ors available at* https://main.sci.gov.in/supremecourt/2020/212/212_2020_31_1503_27229_Judgement_26-Mar-2021.pdf

9. Ibid.

10. Id., Ratan Tata's statement.

Bibliography

Aghor, Ashwin. 'Wadi business clan booked for fraud and cheating in land deal case.' *CatchNews* (29 May 2017). http://www.catchnews.com/india-news/wadia-business-clan-booked-for-fraud-and-cheating-in-land-deal-case-63051.html.

arZan. 'Ratan Tata, India's humble business king.' *Parsi Khabar* (19 May 2009). https://parsikhabar.net/individuals/ratan-tata-indias-humble-business-king/1633/.

Bajaj, Vikas. 'Tata Motors Finds Success in Jaguar Land Rover.' *New York Times* (30 August 2012). http://www.nytimes.com/2012/08/31/business/global/tata-motors-finds-success-in-jaguar-land-rover.html.

Banerjee, Soumyadipta. 'Life was quite a drudgery in my childhood: Ratan Tata.' *DNA* (20 July 2010). http://www.dnaindia.com/lifestyle/report-life-was-quite-a-drudgery-in-my-childhood-ratan-tata-1412192.

Banerji, Sanjay. 'The Noise Around Cyrus Mistry's Firing.' NDTV (1 November 2016). http://www.ndtv.com/opinion/ratan-tata-vs-cyrus-mistry-was-waiting-to-happen-1587210.

Blankenship, Khalid Yahya. *The End of the Jihad State: The Reign of Ibn 'Abd al-Malik and the Collapse of the Umayyads.* Albany: State University of New York Press, 1994.

Casey, Peter. *The World's Greatest Company: The Story of Tata.* Wicklow, Republic of Ireland: Ballpoint Press, 2013.

Cornell University College of Agriculture and Life Sciences. 'Tata-Cornell Institute for Agriculture and Nutrition (TCI).' https://tci.cals.cornell.edu/about.

Cornell University College of Architecture, Art and Planning. 'Ratan Tata '59: The Cornell Story' (2 August 2011). http://www.cornell.edu/video/ratan-tata-the-cornell-story.

Culbert, Regina Vogel. 'Epic Verdict in Trade Secrets Case.' Lexology (21 April 2016). http://www.lexology.com/library/detail.aspx?g=4b4d3d9a-2d85-4e91-b170-9c19f9459e30.

Daily News & Analysis. 'I have always tried to do the "right thing," says Ratan Tata.' *DNA* (7 December 2012). http://www.dnaindia.com/money/interview-i-have-always-tried-to-do-the-right-thing-says-ratan-tata-1774412.

Eduljee, E. K. 'Zoroastrian Demographics: Population, Diaspora, Group Names.' *Zoroastrian Heritage.* http://www.heritageinstitute.com/zoroastrianism/demographics/.

ET Bureau. "Antilla,' Mukesh Ambani's house, shows lack of empathy for poor: Ratan Tata.' *The Times of India* (22 May 2011). http://timesofindia.indiatimes.com/city/mumbai/Antilla-Mukesh-Ambanis-house-shows-lack-of-empathy-for-poor-Ratan-Tata/articleshow/8506287.cms.

Goodstein, Laurie. 'Zoroastrians Keep the Faith, and Keep Dwindling.' *New York Times* (6 September 2006). http://www.nytimes.com/2006/09/06/us/06faith.html.

Graham, Ann. 'Too Good to Fail.' *Strategy + Business*, 23 February 2010, Spring 2010 / Issue 58. http://www. strategy-business.com/article/10106?pg=all.

Harvard Business School. 'Advanced Management Program.' https://www.exed.hbs.edu/programs/amp/Pages/default.aspx?&utm_campaign=USCA%20-%20Brand%20-%20CLP&utm_medium=SEM&utm_source=google&utm_term=advanced%20management%20program%20harvard.

Harvard Business School Communications. 'Business School to dedicate Tata Hall.' *Harvard Gazette* (5 December 2013). http://news.harvard.edu/gazette/story/2013/12/business-school-to-dedicate-tata-hall/.

Hindu Editorial. 'Tata to Corus.' *The Hindu* (1 April 2016). http://www.thehindu.com/opinion/editorial/tata-to-corus/article8418851.ece.

Irani, Mejernaaz Shovir. 'Ratan Tata Addresses Cathedral and John Connon School Alumni.' *Parsi Khabar* (31 March 2009). https://parsikhabar.net/current-affairs/ratan-tata-addresses-cathedral-and-john-connon-school-alumni/1547/.

Iyer, Srividhya. 'Cyrus Mistry fired! Here's all you need to know about who he is and why TATA said tata to its Group Chairman.' *India* (24 October 2016). http://www.india.com/news/india/cyrus-mistry-fired-heres-all-you-need-to-know-about-who-he-is-and-why-tata-said-tata-to-its-group-chairman-1613930/.

Jayanthi, Akanksha. 'Epic asks court to reduce $940M awarded in Tata case.' *Becker's Health IT & CIO Review* (15 June 2016). http://www.

beckershospitalreview.com/healthcare-information-technology/epic-asks-court-to-reduce-940m-awarded-in-tata-case.html.

Kumar, Dharminder. 'How history will come full circle if Tatas buy Air India.' *The Economic Times* (21 June 2017). http://economictimes. indiatimes.com/industry/transportation/airlines-/-aviation/how-history-will-come-full-circle-if-tatas-buy-air-india/articleshowsp/59253577. cms?intenttarget=no&utm_source=newsletter&utm_medium=email&utm_campaign=Dailynewsletter&type=dailynews&ncode=07871b2349381c8f00c b79329d50b27d.

Majumdar, Boria and Nalin Mehta. *India and the Olympics.* New York: Routledge, 2009.

Malik, Aman. 'Who is Ratan Tata and how "real" a Tata is he?' News Corp VCCircle (30 November 2016). http://www.vccircle.com/news/general/2016/11/30/who-ratan-tata-and-how-real-tata-he.

McGrath, Rita. 'Failure Is a Gold Mine for India's Tata.' *Harvard Business Review* (11 April 2011). https://hbr.org/2011/04/failure-is-a-gold-mine-for-ind.

Noronha, Christabelle. 'Treating the Customer as King.' Tata Interviews and Stories (March 2003). http://www.tata.com/aboutus/articlesinside/IY!$$$$!v0UIcUDM=/TLYVr3YPkMU.

Noronha, Christabelle. 'Vision of the future: Group Chairman Ratan Tata speaks on a wide range of issues concerning the Tata group and its place in a world changing more dramatically than ever before.' *Tata: Our Businesses/ Tata Companies/Tata Sons/Interviews and Stories* (August 2006). http://www.tata.com/article/inside/JVypZzs7GuQ=/TLYVr3YPkMU=.

Oxfam International. 'Just 8 men own same wealth as half the world.' Oxfam International blog (16 January 2017). https://www.oxfam.org/en/pressroom/pressreleases/2017-01-16/just-8-men-own-same-wealth-half-world.

Pandathil, Rajesh and Kishor Kadam. 'Tata Steel's failure with Corus and Tata Motors' success with JLR: A tale of 2 buyouts in 9 charts.' FirstPost (1 April 2016). http://www.firstpost.com/business/a-tale-of-2-acquisitions-in-9-charts-tata-steels-failure-with-corus-and-tata-motors-success-with-jlr-2704788.html.

Pazzanese, Christina. 'A new jewel along the river.' *Harvard Gazette* (10 December 2013). http://news.harvard.edu/gazette/story/2013/12/a-new-jewel-along-the-river/.

Piramal, Gita. 'The Reluctant Tycoon.' *The Economic Times* (10 November 1996). http://www.tata.com/article/inside/5SGOjaoiUhU=/TLYVr3YPkMU=.

Piramal, Gita. *Business Maharajas*. New Delhi: Penguin Books India, 1997.

PTI. 'Felt Confused and humiliated during early Harvard days: Ratan Tata.' *The Times of India* (12 December 2013). http://timesofindia.indiatimes.com/india/Felt-confused-and-humiliated-during-early-Harvard-days-Ratan-Tata/articleshow/27238964.cms.

PTI. 'US jury slaps $940 million fine on Tata group in trade secret case.' *The Times of India* (16 April 2016). https://web.archive.org/web/20160416195148/http://timesofindia.indiatimes.com/business/india-business/US-jury-slaps-940-million-fine-on-Tata-group-in-trade-secret-case/articleshow/51853815.cms?

Ramesh, Randeep. 'The Tatas are a reconstructed family. They promote talent rather than blood relations. Ratan was clearly talented.' *Tata: The Guardian Profile* (27 March 2008). https://www.theguardian.com/business/2008/mar/28/automotive.mergersandacquisitions.

Rao, C. Narayana. 'Five Guiding Principles of JRD Tata.' *Inspirational Musings* (10 March 2008). http://wowmusings.blogspot.com/2008/03/five-guiding-principles-of-jrd-tata.html.

Rediff Interview, The. 'Ratan Tata, Chairman, Tata Group.' *Rediff India Abroad* (1 February 2007). http://www.rediff.com/money/2007/feb/01corus5.htm.

Sanghvi, Vir. 'Ratan Tata.' http://www.virsanghvi.com/People-Detail.aspx?Key=3.

Taneja, Shiv. 'Hotting up: Workers intensify agitation.' *India Today* (11 November 1989). http://indiatoday.intoday.in/story/telco-workers-intensify-agitation/1/324104.html.

Tata. 'A life lived from the heart.' *About Us/Heritage/Tata Titans* (April 2004). http://www.tata.com/aboutus/articlesinside/A-life-lived-from-the-heart.

Tata. 'A World to Win.' *Our Businesses/Tata Companies/Tata Sons/Stories* (June 2005). http://tata.com/article/inside/u6rl6KEdYYM%3D/TLYVr3YPkMU%3D.

Tata. 'Celebrating innovation.' Our Businesses . . . Stories (April 2012). http://www.tata.com/article/inside/xqkFEPUqPbE=/TLYVr3YPkMU=.

Tata. 'Dorabji Tata while laying the foundation stone of the Lonavala Dam.' 8 February 1911.' http://www.tata.com/aboutus/articlesinside/FX6UE!$$$$!cbFhc=/TLYVr3YPkMU=.

Tata. 'In the name of the father.' http://www.tata.co.in/aboutus/articlesinside/!$$$!vi!$$$!KywJPS4=/TLYVr3YP-kMU=

Tata. 'The man who played from the heart.' http:// ww.tata.com/aboutus/articlesinside/CPKdkBZjW3c=/TLY- Vr3YPkMU=.

Tata. 'The quotable Jamsetji Tata.' *About Us/Heritage/ Tata Titans* (March 2008). http://www.tata.com/aboutus/articlesinside/The-quotable-Jamsetji-Tata.

Tata Consultancy Services Limited. *Annual Report 2009-10.* http://investors. tcs.com/investors/Documents/Annual%20Reports/TCS_Annual_Report_2009-2010.PDF.

Tirawri, Prateeksha M. *Pride of the Nation: Ratan Tata.* New Delhi: Diamond Books, 2015.

TNN. Tata's Olympic safari.' *Times of India*, 3 August 2008. http:// timesofindia.indiatimes.com/home/stoi/deep-focus/tatas-olympic-safari/ articleshow/3319673.cms.

Vivify Change Catalyst. 'Ratan Tata and NELCO Crucible—the untold story.' *Vivify* (11 October 2013). https://vivifychangecatalyst.wordpress. com/2013/10/11/ratan-tata-and-nelco-crucible-the-untold-story/.

Whitworth, Damien. 'The Empire strikes back.' Reprinted from *The Times Magazine* (27 May 2006) in Tata, 'Our Business.' http://tata.com/article/ inside/7s86!$$$!74eJOU=/TLYVr3YPkMU=.

Witzel, Morgen. *Tata: The Evolution of a Corporate Brand.* New Delhi: Penguin Books India, 2010.

Zachariah, Reeba, and Vipashana V K. 'Jimmy Naval Tata, the brother, a Tata trustee, who lives in the shadows.' *The Times of India* (21 December 2016). https://timesofindia.indiatimes.com/business/india-business/The-brother-a-Tata-trustee-who-lives-in-the-shadows/articleshow/56092362.cms.